WUTHERING HEIGHTS

Emily Brontë

D0031994

SPARK PUBLISHING

© 2002, 2007 by Spark Publishing, A Division of Barnes & Noble

This Spark Publishing edition 2014 by SparkNotes LLC, an Affiliate of Barnes & Noble

All rights reserved. No part of this publication may be reproduced, stored in a retrieval system, or transmitted in any form or by any means (including electronic, mechanical, photocopying, recording, or otherwise) without prior written permission from the publisher.

122 Fifth Avenue
New York, NY 10011
www.sparknotes.com

ISBN 978-1-4114-6971-6

Please submit changes or report errors to www.sparknotes.com/errors.

Printed in Canada

10 9 8 7 6 5 4 3 2 1

Contents

CONTEXT

Wuthering heights, which has long been one of the most popular and highly regarded novels in English literature, seemed to hold little promise when it was published in 1847, selling very poorly and receiving only a few mixed reviews. Victorian readers found the book shocking and inappropriate in its depiction of passionate, ungoverned love and cruelty (despite the fact that the novel portrays no sex or bloodshed), and the work was virtually ignored. Even Emily Brontë's sister Charlotte—an author whose works contained similar motifs of Gothic love and desolate landscapes—remained ambivalent toward the unapologetic intensity of her sister's novel. In a preface to the book, which she wrote shortly after Emily Brontë's death, Charlotte Brontë stated, "Whether it is right or advisable to create beings like Heathcliff, I do not know. I scarcely think it is."

Emily Brontë lived an eccentric, closely guarded life. She was born in 1818, two years after Charlotte and a year and a half before her sister Anne, who also became an author. Her father worked as a church rector, and her aunt, who raised the Brontë children after their mother died, was deeply religious. Emily Brontë did not take to her aunt's Christian fervor; the character of Joseph, a caricature of an evangelical, may have been inspired by her aunt's religiosity. The Brontës lived in Haworth, a Yorkshire village in the midst of the moors. These wild, desolate expanses—later the setting of *Wuthering Heights*—made up the Brontës' daily environment, and Emily lived among them her entire life. She died in 1848, at the age of thirty.

As witnessed by their extraordinary literary accomplishments, the Brontë children were a highly creative group, writing stories, plays, and poems for their own amusement. Largely left to their own devices, the children created imaginary worlds in which to play. Yet the sisters knew that the outside world would not respond favorably to their creative expression; female authors were often treated less seriously than their male counterparts in the nineteenth century. Thus the Brontë sisters thought it best to publish their adult works under assumed names. Charlotte wrote as Currer Bell, Emily as Ellis Bell, and Anne as Acton Bell. Their real identities remained secret until after Emily and Anne had died, when Charlotte at last revealed the truth of their novels' authorship.

Today, *Wuthering Heights* has a secure position in the canon of world literature, and Emily Brontë is revered as one of the finest writers—male or female—of the nineteenth century. Like Charlotte Brontë's *Jane Eyre, Wuthering Heights* is based partly on the Gothic tradition of the late eighteenth century, a style of literature that featured supernatural encounters, crumbling ruins, moonless nights, and grotesque imagery, seeking to create effects of mystery and fear. But *Wuthering Heights* transcends its genre in its sophisticated observation and artistic subtlety. The novel has been studied, analyzed, dissected, and discussed from every imaginable critical perspective, yet it remains unexhausted. And while the novel's symbolism, themes, structure, and language may all spark fertile exploration, the bulk of its popularity may rest on its unforgettable characters. As a shattering presentation of the doomed love affair between the fiercely passionate Catherine and Heathcliff, it remains one of the most haunting love stories in all of literature.

PLOT OVERVIEW

IN THE LATE WINTER MONTHS OF 1801, a man named Lockwood rents a manor house called Thrushcross Grange in the isolated moor country of England. Here, he meets his dour landlord, Heathcliff, a wealthy man who lives in the ancient manor of Wuthering Heights, four miles away from the Grange. In this wild, stormy countryside, Lockwood asks his housekeeper, Nelly Dean, to tell him the story of Heathcliff and the strange denizens of Wuthering Heights. Nelly consents, and Lockwood writes down his recollections of her tale in his diary; these written recollections form the main part of *Wuthering Heights*.

Nelly remembers her childhood. As a young girl, she works as a servant at Wuthering Heights for the owner of the manor, Mr. Earnshaw, and his family. One day, Mr. Earnshaw goes to Liverpool and returns home with an orphan boy whom he will raise with his own children. At first, the Earnshaw children—a boy named Hindley and his younger sister Catherine—detest the dark-skinned Heathcliff. But Catherine quickly comes to love him, and the two soon grow inseparable, spending their days playing on the moors. After his wife's death, Mr. Earnshaw grows to prefer Heathcliff to his own son, and when Hindley continues his cruelty to Heathcliff, Mr. Earnshaw sends Hindley away to college, keeping Heathcliff nearby.

Three years later, Mr. Earnshaw dies, and Hindley inherits Wuthering Heights. He returns with a wife, Frances, and immediately seeks revenge on Heathcliff. Once an orphan, later a pampered and favored son, Heathcliff now finds himself treated as a common laborer, forced to work in the fields. Heathcliff continues his close relationship with Catherine, however. One night they wander to Thrushcross Grange, hoping to tease Edgar and Isabella Linton, the cowardly, snobbish children who live there. Catherine is bitten by a dog and is forced to stay at the Grange to recuperate for five weeks, during which time Mrs. Linton works to make her a proper young lady. By the time Catherine returns, she has become infatuated with Edgar, and her relationship with Heathcliff grows more complicated.

When Frances dies after giving birth to a baby boy named Hareton, Hindley descends into the depths of alcoholism, and behaves even more cruelly and abusively toward Heathcliff. Eventually,

Catherine's desire for social advancement prompts her to become engaged to Edgar Linton, despite her overpowering love for Heathcliff. Heathcliff runs away from Wuthering Heights, staying away for three years, and returning shortly after Catherine and Edgar's marriage.

When Heathcliff returns, he immediately sets about seeking revenge on all who have wronged him. Having come into a vast and mysterious wealth, he deviously lends money to the drunken Hindley, knowing that Hindley will increase his debts and fall into deeper despondency. When Hindley dies, Heathcliff inherits the manor. He also places himself in line to inherit Thrushcross Grange by marrying Isabella Linton, whom he treats very cruelly. Catherine becomes ill, gives birth to a daughter, and dies. Heathcliff begs her spirit to remain on Earth—she may take whatever form she will, she may haunt him, drive him mad—just as long as she does not leave him alone. Shortly thereafter, Isabella flees to London and gives birth to Heathcliff's son, named Linton after her family. She keeps the boy with her there.

Thirteen years pass, during which Nelly Dean serves as Catherine's daughter's nursemaid at Thrushcross Grange. Young Catherine is beautiful and headstrong like her mother, but her temperament is modified by her father's gentler influence. Young Catherine grows up at the Grange with no knowledge of Wuthering Heights; one day, however, wandering through the moors, she discovers the manor, meets Hareton, and plays together with him. Soon afterwards, Isabella dies, and Linton comes to live with Heathcliff. Heathcliff treats his sickly, whining son even more cruelly than he treated the boy's mother.

Three years later, Catherine meets Heathcliff on the moors, and makes a visit to Wuthering Heights to meet Linton. She and Linton begin a secret romance conducted entirely through letters. When Nelly destroys Catherine's collection of letters, the girl begins sneaking out at night to spend time with her frail young lover, who asks her to come back and nurse him back to health. However, it quickly becomes apparent that Linton is pursuing Catherine only because Heathcliff is forcing him to; Heathcliff hopes that if Catherine marries Linton, his legal claim upon Thrushcross Grange—and his revenge upon Edgar Linton—will be complete. One day, as Edgar Linton grows ill and nears death, Heathcliff lures Nelly and Catherine back to Wuthering Heights, and holds them prisoner until Catherine marries Linton. Soon after the mar-

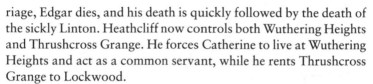

riage, Edgar dies, and his death is quickly followed by the death of the sickly Linton. Heathcliff now controls both Wuthering Heights and Thrushcross Grange. He forces Catherine to live at Wuthering Heights and act as a common servant, while he rents Thrushcross Grange to Lockwood.

Nelly's story ends as she reaches the present. Lockwood, appalled, ends his tenancy at Thrushcross Grange and returns to London. However, six months later, he pays a visit to Nelly, and learns of further developments in the story. Although Catherine originally mocked Hareton's ignorance and illiteracy (in an act of retribution, Heathcliff ended Hareton's education after Hindley died), Catherine grows to love Hareton as they live together at Wuthering Heights. Heathcliff becomes more and more obsessed with the memory of the elder Catherine, to the extent that he begins speaking to her ghost. Everything he sees reminds him of her. Shortly after a night spent walking on the moors, Heathcliff dies. Hareton and young Catherine inherit Wuthering Heights and Thrushcross Grange, and they plan to be married on the next New Year's Day. After hearing the end of the story, Lockwood goes to visit the graves of Catherine and Heathcliff.

CHRONOLOGY

The story of *Wuthering Heights* is told through flashbacks recorded in diary entries, and events are often presented out of chronological order—Lockwood's narrative takes place after Nelly's narrative, for instance, but is interspersed with Nelly's story in his journal. Nevertheless, the novel contains enough clues to enable an approximate reconstruction of its chronology, which was elaborately designed by Emily Brontë. For instance, Lockwood's diary entries are recorded in the late months of 1801 and in September 1802; in 1801, Nelly tells Lockwood that she has lived at Thrushcross Grange for eighteen years, since Catherine's marriage to Edgar, which must then have occurred in 1783. We know that Catherine was engaged to Edgar for three years, and that Nelly was twenty-two when they were engaged, so the engagement must have taken place in 1780, and Nelly must have been born in 1758. Since Nelly is a few years older than Catherine, and since Lockwood comments that Heathcliff is about forty years old in 1801, it stands to reason that Heathcliff and Catherine were born around 1761, three years after Nelly. There are several other clues like this in the novel (such as Hareton's birth, which occurs in June, 1778). The following chronology is based on those clues, and should closely approximate the timing of the novel's important events. A "~" before a date indicates that it cannot be precisely determined from the evidence in the novel, but only closely estimated.

1500	The stone above the front door of Wuthering Heights, bearing the name of Hareton Earnshaw, is inscribed, possibly to mark the completion of the house.
1758	Nelly is born.
~1761	Heathcliff and Catherine are born.
~1767	Mr. Earnshaw brings Heathcliff to live at Wuthering Heights.
1774	Mr. Earnshaw sends Hindley away to college.
1777	Mr. Earnshaw dies; Hindley and Frances take possession of Wuthering Heights; Catherine first visits Thrushcross Grange around Christmastime.
1778	Hareton is born in June; Frances dies; Hindley begins his slide into alcoholism.
1780	Catherine becomes engaged to Edgar Linton; Heathcliff leaves Wuthering Heights.
1783	Catherine and Edgar are married; Heathcliff arrives at Thrushcross Grange in September.
1784	Heathcliff and Isabella elope in the early part of the year; Catherine becomes ill with brain fever; young Catherine is born late in the year; Catherine dies.
1785	Early in the year, Isabella flees Wuthering Heights and settles in London; Linton is born.
~1785	Hindley dies; Heathcliff inherits Wuthering Heights.

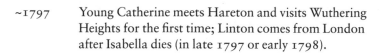

~1797   Young Catherine meets Hareton and visits Wuthering Heights for the first time; Linton comes from London after Isabella dies (in late 1797 or early 1798).

1800   Young Catherine stages her romance with Linton in the winter.

1801   Early in the year, young Catherine is imprisoned by Heathcliff and forced to marry Linton; Edgar Linton dies; Linton dies; Heathcliff assumes control of Thrushcross Grange. Late in the year, Lockwood rents the Grange from Heathcliff and begins his tenancy. In a winter storm, Lockwood takes ill and begins conversing with Nelly Dean.

1801–1802 During the winter, Nelly narrates her story for Lockwood.

1802   In spring, Lockwood returns to London; Catherine and Hareton fall in love; Heathcliff dies; Lockwood returns in September and hears the end of the story from Nelly.

1803   On New Year's Day, young Catherine and Hareton plan to be married.

CHARACTER LIST

Heathcliff An orphan brought to live at Wuthering Heights by Mr. Earnshaw, Heathcliff falls into an intense, unbreakable love with Mr. Earnshaw's daughter Catherine. After Mr. Earnshaw dies, his resentful son Hindley abuses Heathcliff and treats him as a servant. Because of her desire for social prominence, Catherine marries Edgar Linton instead of Heathcliff. Heathcliff's humiliation and misery prompt him to spend most of the rest of his life seeking revenge on Hindley, his beloved Catherine, and their respective children (Hareton and young Catherine). A powerful, fierce, and often cruel man, Heathcliff acquires a fortune and uses his extraordinary powers of will to acquire both Wuthering Heights and Thrushcross Grange, the estate of Edgar Linton.

Catherine The daughter of Mr. Earnshaw and his wife, Catherine falls powerfully in love with Heathcliff, the orphan Mr. Earnshaw brings home from Liverpool. Catherine loves Heathcliff so intensely that she claims they are the same person. However, her desire for social advancement motivates her to marry Edgar Linton instead. Catherine is free-spirited, beautiful, spoiled, and often arrogant. She is given to fits of temper, and she is torn between her wild passion for Heathcliff and her social ambition. She brings misery to both of the men who love her.

Edgar Linton Well-bred but rather spoiled as a boy, Edgar Linton grows into a tender, constant, but cowardly man. He is almost the ideal gentleman: Catherine accurately describes him as "handsome," "pleasant to be with," "cheerful," and "rich." However, this full assortment of gentlemanly characteristics, along with his civilized virtues, proves useless in Edgar's clashes with his foil, Heathcliff, who gains power over his wife, sister, and daughter.

Nelly Dean   Nelly Dean (known formally as Ellen Dean) serves as the chief narrator of *Wuthering Heights*. A sensible, intelligent, and compassionate woman, she grew up essentially alongside Hindley and Catherine Earnshaw and is deeply involved in the story she tells. She has strong feelings for the characters in her story, and these feelings complicate her narration.

Lockwood   Lockwood's narration forms a frame around Nelly's; he serves as an intermediary between Nelly and the reader. A somewhat vain and presumptuous gentleman, he deals very clumsily with the inhabitants of Wuthering Heights. Lockwood comes from a more domesticated region of England, and he finds himself at a loss when he witnesses the strange household's disregard for the social conventions that have always structured his world. As a narrator, his vanity and unfamiliarity with the story occasionally lead him to misunderstand events.

Young Catherine   For clarity's sake, this SparkNote refers to the daughter of Edgar Linton and the first Catherine as "young Catherine." The first Catherine begins her life as Catherine Earnshaw and ends it as Catherine Linton; her daughter begins as Catherine Linton and, assuming that she marries Hareton after the end of the story, goes on to become Catherine Earnshaw. The mother and the daughter share not only a name, but also a tendency toward headstrong behavior, impetuousness, and occasional arrogance. However, Edgar's influence seems to have tempered young Catherine's character, and she is a gentler and more compassionate creature than her mother.

Hareton Earnshaw   The son of Hindley and Frances Earnshaw, Hareton is Catherine's nephew. After Hindley's death, Heathcliff assumes custody of Hareton, and raises him as an uneducated field worker, just as Hindley had done to Heathcliff himself. Thus Heathcliff uses Hareton to seek revenge on Hindley. Illiterate and quick-tempered, Hareton is easily humiliated, but shows a good heart and a deep desire to improve himself. At the end of the novel, he marries young Catherine.

Linton Heathcliff Heathcliff's son by Isabella. Weak, sniveling, demanding, and constantly ill, Linton is raised in London by his mother and does not meet his father until he is thirteen years old, when he goes to live with him after his mother's death. Heathcliff despises Linton, treats him contemptuously, and, by forcing him to marry the young Catherine, uses him to cement his control over Thrushcross Grange after Edgar Linton's death. Linton himself dies not long after this marriage.

Hindley Earnshaw Catherine's brother, and Mr. Earnshaw's son. Hindley resents it when Heathcliff is brought to live at Wuthering Heights. After his father dies and he inherits the estate, Hindley begins to abuse the young Heathcliff, terminating his education and forcing him to work in the fields. When Hindley's wife Frances dies shortly after giving birth to their son Hareton, he lapses into alcoholism and dissipation.

Isabella Linton Edgar Linton's sister, who falls in love with Heathcliff and marries him. She sees Heathcliff as a romantic figure, like a character in a novel. Ultimately, she ruins her life by falling in love with him. He never returns her feelings and treats her as a mere tool in his quest for revenge on the Linton family.

Mr. Earnshaw Catherine and Hindley's father. Mr. Earnshaw adopts Heathcliff and brings him to live at Wuthering Heights. Mr. Earnshaw prefers Heathcliff to Hindley but nevertheless bequeaths Wuthering Heights to Hindley when he dies.

Mrs. Earnshaw Catherine and Hindley's mother, who neither likes nor trusts the orphan Heathcliff when he is brought to live at her house. She dies shortly after Heathcliff's arrival at Wuthering Heights.

CHARACTER LIST

Joseph   A long-winded, fanatically religious, elderly servant at Wuthering Heights. Joseph is strange, stubborn, and unkind, and he speaks with a thick Yorkshire accent.

Frances Earnshaw Hindley's simpering, silly wife, who treats Heathcliff cruelly. She dies shortly after giving birth to Hareton.

Mr. Linton Edgar and Isabella's father and the proprietor of Thrushcross Grange when Heathcliff and Catherine are children. An established member of the gentry, he raises his son and daughter to be well-mannered young people.

Mrs. Linton Mr. Linton's somewhat snobbish wife, who does not like Heathcliff to be allowed near her children, Edgar and Isabella. She teaches Catherine to act like a gentle-woman, thereby instilling her with social ambitions.

Zillah   The housekeeper at Wuthering Heights during the latter stages of the narrative.

Mr. Green Edgar Linton's lawyer, who arrives too late to hear Edgar's final instruction to change his will, which would have prevented Heathcliff from obtaining control over Thrushcross Grange.

ANALYSIS OF MAJOR CHARACTERS

HEATHCLIFF

Wuthering Heights centers around the story of Heathcliff. The first paragraph of the novel provides a vivid physical picture of him, as Lockwood describes how his "black eyes" withdraw suspiciously under his brows at Lockwood's approach. Nelly's story begins with his introduction into the Earnshaw family, his vengeful machinations drive the entire plot, and his death ends the book. The desire to understand him and his motivations has kept countless readers engaged in the novel.

Heathcliff, however, defies being understood, and it is difficult for readers to resist seeing what they want or expect to see in him. The novel teases the reader with the possibility that Heathcliff is something other than what he seems—that his cruelty is merely an expression of his frustrated love for Catherine, or that his sinister behaviors serve to conceal the heart of a romantic hero. We expect Heathcliff's character to contain such a hidden virtue because he resembles a hero in a romance novel. Traditionally, romance novel heroes appear dangerous, brooding, and cold at first, only later to emerge as fiercely devoted and loving. One hundred years before Emily Brontë wrote *Wuthering Heights*, the notion that "a reformed rake makes the best husband" was already a cliché of romantic literature, and romance novels center around the same cliché to this day.

However, Heathcliff does not reform, and his malevolence proves so great and long-lasting that it cannot be adequately explained even as a desire for revenge against Hindley, Catherine, Edgar, etc. As he himself points out, his abuse of Isabella is purely sadistic, as he amuses himself by seeing how much abuse she can take and still come cringing back for more. Critic Joyce Carol Oates argues that Emily Brontë does the same thing to the reader that Heathcliff does to Isabella, testing to see how many times the reader can be shocked by Heathcliff's gratuitous violence and still, masochistically, insist on seeing him as a romantic hero.

It is significant that Heathcliff begins his life as a homeless orphan on the streets of Liverpool. When Brontë composed her book, in the 1840s, the English economy was severely depressed, and the conditions of the factory workers in industrial areas like Liverpool were so appalling that the upper and middle classes feared violent revolt. Thus, many of the more affluent members of society beheld these workers with a mixture of sympathy and fear. In literature, the smoky, threatening, miserable factory-towns were often represented in religious terms, and compared to hell. The poet William Blake, writing near the turn of the nineteenth century, speaks of England's "dark Satanic Mills." Heathcliff, of course, is frequently compared to a demon by the other characters in the book.

Considering this historical context, Heathcliff seems to embody the anxieties that the book's upper- and middle-class audience had about the working classes. The reader may easily sympathize with him when he is powerless, as a child tyrannized by Hindley Earnshaw, but he becomes a villain when he acquires power and returns to Wuthering Heights with money and the trappings of a gentleman. This corresponds with the ambivalence the upper classes felt toward the lower classes—the upper classes had charitable impulses toward lower-class citizens when they were miserable, but feared the prospect of the lower classes trying to escape their miserable circumstances by acquiring political, social, cultural, or economic power.

CATHERINE

The location of Catherine's coffin symbolizes the conflict that tears apart her short life. She is not buried in the chapel with the Lintons. Nor is her coffin placed among the tombs of the Earnshaws. Instead, as Nelly describes in Chapter XVI, Catherine is buried "in a corner of the kirkyard, where the wall is so low that heath and bilberry plants have climbed over it from the moor." Moreover, she is buried with Edgar on one side and Heathcliff on the other, suggesting her conflicted loyalties. Her actions are driven in part by her social ambitions, which initially are awakened during her first stay at the Lintons', and which eventually compel her to marry Edgar. However, she is also motivated by impulses that prompt her to violate social conventions—to love Heathcliff, throw temper tantrums, and run around on the moor.

Isabella Linton—Catherine's sister-in-law and Heathcliff's wife, who was born in the same year that Catherine was—serves as

Catherine's foil. The two women's parallel positions allow us to see their differences with greater clarity. Catherine represents wild nature, in both her high, lively spirits and her occasional cruelty, whereas Isabella represents culture and civilization, both in her refinement and in her weakness.

EDGAR

Just as Isabella Linton serves as Catherine's foil, Edgar Linton serves as Heathcliff's. Edgar is born and raised a gentleman. He is graceful, well-mannered, and instilled with civilized virtues. These qualities cause Catherine to choose Edgar over Heathcliff and thus to initiate the contention between the men. Nevertheless, Edgar's gentlemanly qualities ultimately prove useless in his ensuing rivalry with Heathcliff. Edgar is particularly humiliated by his confrontation with Heathcliff in Chapter XI, in which he openly shows his fear of fighting Heathcliff. Catherine, having witnessed the scene, taunts him, saying, "Heathcliff would as soon lift a finger at you as the king would march his army against a colony of mice." As the reader can see from the earliest descriptions of Edgar as a spoiled child, his refinement is tied to his helplessness and impotence.

Charlotte Brontë, in her preface to the 1850 edition of *Wuthering Heights,* refers to Edgar as "an example of constancy and tenderness," and goes on to suggest that her sister Emily was using Edgar to point out that such characteristics constitute true virtues in all human beings, and not just in women, as society tended to believe. However, Charlotte's reading seems influenced by her own feminist agenda. Edgar's inability to counter Heathcliff's vengeance, and his naïve belief on his deathbed in his daughter's safety and happiness, make him a weak, if sympathetic, character.

THEMES, MOTIFS & SYMBOLS

THEMES

Themes are the fundamental and often universal ideas explored in a literary work.

THE DESTRUCTIVENESS OF A LOVE THAT NEVER CHANGES

Catherine and Heathcliff's passion for one another seems to be the center of *Wuthering Heights,* given that it is stronger and more lasting than any other emotion displayed in the novel, and that it is the source of most of the major conflicts that structure the novel's plot. As she tells Catherine and Heathcliff's story, Nelly criticizes both of them harshly, condemning their passion as immoral, but this passion is obviously one of the most compelling and memorable aspects of the book. It is not easy to decide whether Brontë intends the reader to condemn these lovers as blameworthy or to idealize them as romantic heroes whose love transcends social norms and conventional morality. The book is actually structured around two parallel love stories, the first half of the novel centering on the love between Catherine and Heathcliff, while the less dramatic second half features the developing love between young Catherine and Hareton. In contrast to the first, the latter tale ends happily, restoring peace and order to Wuthering Heights and Thrushcross Grange. The differences between the two love stories contribute to the reader's understanding of why each ends the way it does.

The most important feature of young Catherine and Hareton's love story is that it involves growth and change. Early in the novel Hareton seems irredeemably brutal, savage, and illiterate, but over time he becomes a loyal friend to young Catherine and learns to read. When young Catherine first meets Hareton he seems completely alien to her world, yet her attitude also evolves from contempt to love. Catherine and Heathcliff's love, on the other hand, is rooted in their childhood and is marked by the refusal to change. In choosing to marry Edgar, Catherine seeks a more genteel life, but she refuses to adapt to her role as wife, either by sacrificing Heathcliff or embracing Edgar. In Chapter XII she suggests to Nelly that the years since she was twelve years old and her father died have been like a blank to her, and she longs to return to the moors of her childhood. Heathcliff, for his part, possesses a seemingly superhuman ability to maintain the same attitude and to nurse the same grudges over many years.

Moreover, Catherine and Heathcliff's love is based on their shared perception that they are identical. Catherine declares, famously, "I *am* Heathcliff," while Heathcliff, upon Catherine's death, wails that he cannot live without his "soul," meaning Catherine. Their love denies difference, and is strangely asexual. The two do not kiss in dark corners or arrange secret trysts, as adulterers do. Given that Catherine and Heathcliff's love is based upon their refusal to change over time or embrace difference in others, it is fitting that the disastrous problems of their generation are overcome not by some climactic reversal, but simply by the inexorable passage of time, and the rise of a new and distinct generation. Ultimately, *Wuthering Heights* presents a vision of life as a process of change, and celebrates this process over and against the romantic intensity of its principal characters.

The Precariousness of Social Class

As members of the gentry, the Earnshaws and the Lintons occupy a somewhat precarious place within the hierarchy of late eighteenth- and early nineteenth-century British society. At the top of British society was the royalty, followed by the aristocracy, then by the gentry, and then by the lower classes, who made up the vast majority of the population. Although the gentry, or upper middle class, possessed servants and often large estates, they held a nonetheless fragile social position. The social status of aristocrats was a formal and settled matter, because aristocrats had official titles. Members of the gentry, however, held no titles, and their status was thus subject to change. A man might see himself as a gentleman but find, to his embarrassment, that his neighbors did not share this view. A discussion of whether or not a man was really a gentleman would consider such questions as how much land he owned, how many tenants and servants he had, how he spoke, whether he kept horses and a carriage, and whether his money came from land or "trade"—gentlemen scorned banking and commercial activities.

Considerations of class status often crucially inform the characters' motivations in *Wuthering Heights*. Catherine's decision to marry Edgar so that she will be "the greatest woman of the neighborhood" is only the most obvious example. The Lintons are relatively firm in their gentry status but nonetheless take great pains to prove this status through their behaviors. The Earnshaws, on the other hand, rest on much shakier ground socially. They do not have a carriage, they have less land, and their house, as Lockwood remarks with great puzzlement, resembles that of a "homely, northern farmer" and not that of a gentleman. The shifting nature of social status is demonstrated most strikingly in Heathcliff's trajectory from homeless waif to young gentleman-by-adoption to common laborer to gentleman again (although the status-conscious Lockwood remarks that Heathcliff is only a gentleman in "dress and manners").

MOTIFS

Motifs are recurring structures, contrasts, and literary devices that can help to develop and inform the text's major themes.

DOUBLES

Brontë organizes her novel by arranging its elements—characters, places, and themes—into pairs. Catherine and Heathcliff are closely matched in many ways, and see themselves as identical. Catherine's character is divided into two warring sides: the side that wants Edgar and the side that wants Heathcliff. Catherine and young Catherine are both remarkably similar and strikingly different. The two houses, Wuthering Heights and Thrushcross Grange, represent opposing worlds and values. The novel has not one but two distinctly different narrators, Nelly and Mr. Lockwood. The relation between such paired elements is usually quite complicated, with the members of each pair being neither exactly alike nor diametrically opposed. For instance, the Lintons and the Earnshaws may at first seem to represent opposing sets of values, but, by the end of the novel, so many intermarriages have taken place that one can no longer distinguish between the two families.

REPETITION

Repetition is another tactic Brontë employs in organizing *Wuthering Heights*. It seems that nothing ever ends in the world of this novel. Instead, time seems to run in cycles, and the horrors of the past repeat themselves in the present. The way that the names of the characters are recycled, so that the names of the characters of the younger generation seem only to be rescramblings of the names of their parents, leads the reader to consider how plot elements also repeat themselves. For instance, Heathcliff's degradation of Hareton repeats Hindley's degradation of Heathcliff. Also, the young Catherine's mockery of Joseph's earnest evangelical zealousness repeats her mother's. Even Heathcliff's second try at opening Catherine's grave repeats his first.

THE CONFLICT BETWEEN NATURE AND CULTURE

In *Wuthering Heights,* Brontë constantly plays nature and culture against each other. Nature is represented by the Earnshaw family, and by Catherine and Heathcliff in particular. These characters are governed by their passions, not by reflection or ideals of civility. Correspondingly, the house where they live—Wuthering Heights—comes to symbolize a similar wildness. On the other hand, Thrushcross Grange and the Linton family represent culture, refinement, convention, and cultivation.

When, in Chapter VI, Catherine is bitten by the Lintons' dog and brought into Thrushcross Grange, the two sides are brought onto the collision course that structures the majority of the novel's plot. At the time of that first meeting between the Linton and Earnshaw households, chaos has already begun to erupt at Wuthering Heights, where Hindley's cruelty and injustice reign, whereas all seems to be fine and peaceful at Thrushcross Grange. However, the influence of Wuthering Heights soon proves overpowering, and the inhabitants of Thrushcross Grange are drawn into Catherine, Hindley, and Heathcliff's drama. Thus the reader almost may interpret Wuthering Heights's impact on the Linton family as an allegory for the corruption of culture by nature, creating a curious reversal of the more traditional story of the corruption of nature by culture. However, Brontë tells her story in such a way as to prevent our interest and sympathy from straying too far from the wilder characters, and often portrays the more civilized characters as despicably weak and silly. This method of characterization prevents the novel from flattening out into a simple privileging of culture over nature, or vice versa. Thus in the end the reader must acknowledge that the novel is no mere allegory.

Symbols

Symbols are objects, characters, figures, and colors used to represent abstract ideas or concepts.

Moors

The constant emphasis on landscape within the text of *Wuthering Heights* endows the setting with symbolic importance. This landscape is comprised primarily of moors: wide, wild expanses, high but somewhat soggy, and thus infertile. Moorland cannot be cultivated, and its uniformity makes navigation difficult. It features particularly waterlogged patches in which people could potentially drown. (This possibility is mentioned several times in *Wuthering Heights*.) Thus, the moors serve very well as symbols of the wild threat posed by nature. As the setting for the beginnings of Catherine and Heathcliff's bond (the two play on the moors during childhood), the moorland transfers its symbolic associations onto the love affair.

Ghosts

Ghosts appear throughout *Wuthering Heights,* as they do in most other works of Gothic fiction, yet Brontë always presents them in such a way that whether they really exist remains ambiguous. Thus the world of the novel can always be interpreted as a realistic one. Certain ghosts—such as Catherine's spirit when it appears to Lockwood in Chapter III—may be explained as nightmares. The villagers' alleged sightings of Heathcliff's ghost in Chapter XXXIV could be dismissed as unverified superstition. Whether or not the ghosts are "real," they symbolize the manifestation of the past within the present, and the way memory stays with people, permeating their day-to-day lives.

Summary & Analysis

Chapters I–V

Summary: Chapter I

> *But Mr. Heathcliff forms a singular contrast to his*
> *abode and style of living. He is a dark-skinned gypsy in*
> *aspect, in dress and manners a gentleman. . . .*
> *(See* quotations, *p. 53)*

Writing in his diary in 1801, Lockwood describes his first days as a tenant at Thrushcross Grange, an isolated manor in thinly populated Yorkshire. Shortly after arriving at the Grange, he pays a visit to his landlord, Mr. Heathcliff, a surly, dark man living in a manor called Wuthering Heights—"wuthering" being a local adjective used to describe the fierce and wild winds that blow during storms on the moors. During the visit, Heathcliff seems not to trust Lockwood, and leaves him alone in a room with a group of snarling dogs. Lockwood is saved from the hounds by a ruddy-cheeked housekeeper. When Heathcliff returns, Lockwood is angry, but eventually warms toward his taciturn host, and—though he hardly feels that he has been welcomed at Wuthering Heights—he volunteers to visit again the next day.

Summary: Chapter II

On a chilly afternoon not long after his first visit, Lockwood plans to lounge before the fire in his study, but he finds a servant dustily sweeping out the fireplace there, so instead he makes the four-mile walk to Wuthering Heights, arriving just as a light snow begins to fall. He knocks, but no one lets him in, and Joseph, an old servant who speaks with a thick Yorkshire accent, calls out from the barn that Heathcliff is not in the house. Eventually a rough-looking young man comes to let him in, and Lockwood goes into a sitting room where he finds a beautiful girl seated beside a fire. Lockwood assumes she is Heathcliff's wife. He tries to make conversation, but she responds rudely. When Heathcliff arrives, he corrects Lockwood: the young woman is his daughter-in-law. Lockwood then assumes that the young man who let him in must be Heathcliff's son. Heathcliff corrects him again. The young man, Hareton Earnshaw, is not his son, and the girl is the widow of Heathcliff's dead son.

The snowfall becomes a blizzard, and when Lockwood is ready to leave, he is forced to ask for a guide back to Thrushcross Grange. No one will help him. He takes a lantern and says that he will find his own way, promising to return with the lantern in the morning. Joseph, seeing him make his way through the snow, assumes that he is stealing the lantern, and looses the dogs on him. Pinned down by the dogs, Lockwood grows furious, and begins cursing the inhabitants of the house. His anger brings on a nosebleed, and he is forced to stay at Wuthering Heights. The housekeeper, Zillah, leads him to bed.

SUMMARY: CHAPTER III

> *Catherine Earnshaw ... Catherine Heathcliff ...*
> *Catherine Linton. ... a glare of white letters started*
> *from the dark, as vivid as spectres—the air swarmed*
> *with Catherines. ...* (See QUOTATIONS, *p. 54)*

Zillah leads Lockwood to an out-of-the-way room from which Heathcliff has forbidden all visitors. He notices that someone has scratched words into the paint on the ledge by the bed. Three names are inscribed there repeatedly: *Catherine Earnshaw, Catherine Linton,* and *Catherine Heathcliff.* He also finds a diary written approximately twenty-five years earlier. Apparently the diary belonged to Catherine Earnshaw, and Lockwood reads an entry that describes a day at Wuthering Heights shortly after her father died, during which her cruel older brother Hindley forces her and Heathcliff to endure Joseph's tedious sermons. Catherine and Heathcliff seem to have been very close, and Hindley seems to have hated Heathcliff. The diary even describes Hindley telling his wife, Frances, to pull the boy's hair.

Lockwood falls asleep and enters into a pair of nightmares. He awakes from the second when the cone from a fir branch begins tapping on his window. Still half asleep, he attempts to break off the branch by forcing his hand through the window glass. But instead of a branch, he finds a ghostly hand, which seizes his own, and a voice, sobbing the name Catherine Linton, demands to be let in. To free himself, Lockwood rubs the ghost's wrist on the broken glass until blood covers the bed sheets. The ghost releases him, and Lockwood tries to cover the hole in the window with a pile of books. But the books begin to fall, and he cries out in terror. Heathcliff rushes into the room, and Lockwood cries out that the room is haunted.

Heathcliff curses him, but, as Lockwood flees from the room, Heathcliff cries out to Catherine, begging her to return. There are no signs that the ghost was ever at the window. In the morning, Heathcliff treats his daughter-in-law cruelly. He later escorts Lockwood home, where the servants, who believed their master dead in the storm, receive him with joy. Lockwood, however, retreats into his study to escape human company.

Summary: Chapter IV

Having rejected human contact the day before, Lockwood now becomes lonely. When his housekeeper, Nelly Dean, brings him his supper, he bids her sit and tell him the history of the people at Wuthering Heights. She attempts to clarify the family relationships, explaining that the young Catherine whom Lockwood met at Wuthering Heights is the daughter of the Catherine who was Nelly's first mistress at Wuthering Heights, and that Hareton Earnshaw is young Catherine's cousin, the nephew of the first Catherine. The first Catherine was the daughter of Mr. Earnshaw, the late proprietor of Wuthering Heights. Now young Catherine is the last of the Lintons, and Hareton is the last of the Earnshaws. Nelly says that she grew up as a servant at Wuthering Heights, alongside Catherine and her brother Hindley, Mr. Earnshaw's children.

Nelly continues by telling the story of her early years at Wuthering Heights. When Catherine and Hindley are young children, Mr. Earnshaw takes a trip to Liverpool and returns home with a scraggly orphan whom the Earnshaws christen "Heathcliff." Mr. Earnshaw announces that Heathcliff will be raised as a member of the family. Both Catherine and Hindley resent Heathcliff at first, but Catherine quickly grows to love him. Catherine and Heathcliff become inseparable, and Hindley, who continues to treat Heathcliff cruelly, falls into disfavor with his family. Mrs. Earnshaw continues to distrust Heathcliff, but Mr. Earnshaw comes to love the boy more than his own son. When Mrs. Earnshaw dies only two years after Heathcliff's arrival at Wuthering Heights, Hindley is essentially left without an ally.

Summary: Chapter V

Time passes, and Mr. Earnshaw grows frail and weak. Disgusted by the conflict between Heathcliff and Hindley, he sends Hindley away to college. Joseph's fanatical religious beliefs appeal to Mr. Earnshaw as he nears the end of his life, and the old servant exerts more and more sway over his master. Soon, however, Mr. Earnshaw dies, and it is now Catherine and Heathcliff who turn to religion for comfort. They discuss the idea of heaven while awaiting the return of Hindley, who will now be master of Wuthering Heights.

ANALYSIS: CHAPTERS I–V

The strange, deliberately confusing opening chapters of *Wuthering Heights* serve as Brontë's introduction to the world of the novel and to the complex relationships among the characters, as well as to the peculiar style of narration through which the story will be told. One of the most important aspects of the novel is its second- and third-hand manner of narration. Nothing is ever related simply from the perspective of a single participant. Instead, the story is told through entries in Lockwood's diary, but Lockwood does not participate in the events he records. The vast majority of the novel represents Lockwood's written recollections of what he has learned from the testaments of others, whether he is transcribing what he recalls of Catherine's diary entry or recording his conversations with Nelly Dean. Because of the distance that this imposes between the reader and the story itself, it is extremely important to remember that nothing in the book is written from the perspective of an unbiased narrator, and it is often necessary to read between the lines in order to understand events.

The reader can immediately question Lockwood's reliability as a conveyer of facts. A vain and somewhat shallow man, he frequently makes amusing mistakes—he assumes, for instance, that Heathcliff is a gentleman with a house full of servants, even though it is apparent to the reader that Heathcliff is a rough and cruel man with a house full of dogs. Nelly Dean is more knowledgeable about events, as she has participated in many of them first hand, yet while this makes her more trustworthy in some ways, it also makes her more biased in others. She frequently glosses over her own role in the story's developments, particularly when she has behaved badly. Later in the novel, she describes how she took the young Linton to live with his cruel father after the death of his mother. She lies to the boy on the journey, telling him that his father is a kind man, and, after his horrible meeting with Heathcliff, she tries to sneak out when he is not paying attention. He notices her and begs her not to leave him with Heathcliff. She ignores his entreaties, however, and tells Lockwood that she simply had "no excuse for lingering longer." Nelly is generally a dependable source of information, but moments such as this one—and there are many—remind the reader that the story is told by a fallible human being.

Apart from establishing the manner and quality of narration, the most important function of these early chapters is to pique the reader's curiosity about the strange histories of the denizens of Wuthering Heights. The family relationships, including multiple Earnshaws, Catherines, Lintons, and Heathcliffs, seem at this point in the novel to intertwine with baffling complexity, and the characters, because Lockwood first encounters them late in their story, seem full of mysterious passions and ancient, hidden resentments. Even the setting of this history seems to possess its own secrets. Wild and desolate, full of eerie winds and forgotten corners, the land has borne witness to its residents' nighttime walks, forbidden meetings, and graveyard visits. Indeed, the mysteries of the land cannot be separated from the mysteries of the characters, and the physical landscape of the novel is often used to reflect the mental and emotional landscapes of those who live there.

While the odd characters and wild setting contribute to a certain sense of mystery, this sense is most definitively established by the appearance of Catherine Earnshaw's ghost. Yet while Lockwood's account of the event greatly influences the feel of the novel, and while his subsequent account of it to Heathcliff provokes a reaction that may offer us clues as to his relationship with the late Catherine, the reader may still conclude that the ghost is a figment of Lockwood's imagination. Because Lockwood has proven himself flighty and emotional, and he is still half asleep when he encounters the ghost, one could infer that he never actually sees a ghost, but simply has an intense vision in the midst of his dream. It seems likely, however, that Emily Brontë would have intended the ghost to seem real to her readers: such a supernatural phenomenon would certainly be in keeping with the Gothic tone pervading the rest of the novel. Moreover, Heathcliff refers to Catherine's ghost several times during the course of the novel. Clearly he concurs with Lockwood in believing that she haunts Wuthering Heights. Thus the ghost, whether objectively "real" or not, attests to the way the characters remain haunted by a troubling and turbulent past.

CHAPTERS VI–IX

SUMMARY: CHAPTER VI

Hindley and his new wife, a simpering, silly woman named Frances, return to Wuthering Heights in time for Mr. Earnshaw's funeral. Hindley immediately begins to take his revenge on Heathcliff, declaring that Heathcliff no longer will be allowed an education and instead will spend his days working in the fields like a common laborer. But, for the most part, Catherine and Heathcliff are able to escape Hindley's notice, and when Heathcliff is free from his responsibilities they go off onto the moors together to play.

One evening, when Heathcliff and Catherine disappear, Hindley orders that the doors be bolted and that the children not be allowed into the house. Despite his charge, Nelly waits for them, and receives a shock when Heathcliff returns alone. He tells her that he and Catherine made the trip to Thrushcross Grange to spy on and tease Edgar and Isabella Linton, Mr. Linton's children. Before they could succeed in their mission, Skulker, the Lintons' guard dog, took them by surprise and chased them, biting Catherine's ankle. Unable to return home, Catherine was taken inside Thrushcross Grange by a servant. However, the Lintons, repelled by Heathcliff's rough appearance, forbade her playmate to stay with her. The following day, Mr. Linton pays a visit to Wuthering Heights to explain matters to Hindley and upbraids the young man for his mismanagement of Catherine. After Mr. Linton leaves, the humiliated Hindley furiously tells Heathcliff that he may have no further contact with Catherine.

Summary: Chapter VII

Catherine spends five weeks recuperating at the Grange. Mrs. Linton determines to transform the girl into a young lady and spends her time educating Catherine in manners and social graces. Catherine returns to Wuthering Heights at Christmastime, wearing a lovely dress. Hindley says that Heathcliff may greet Catherine "like the other servants," and, when he does so, she says he is dirty in comparison with the Linton children, to whom she has grown accustomed. Heathcliff's feelings are wounded, and he storms out of the room, declaring that he will be as dirty as he likes. The Linton children come for dinner at Wuthering Heights the next day. Nelly helps Heathcliff to wash himself and put on suitable clothes after the boy declares his intention to be "good," but Mrs. Linton has allowed Edgar and Isabella to attend under the condition that Heathcliff be kept away from them. Accordingly, Hindley orders that Heathcliff be locked in the attic until the end of dinner. Before the boy can be locked away, however, Edgar makes a comment about Heathcliff's hair, and Heathcliff angrily flings hot applesauce in his face. Catherine clearly appears unhappy with Hindley's treatment of Heathcliff, and after dinner she goes up to see him. Nelly frees the boy and gives him some supper in the kitchen. Heathcliff confides to Nelly that he intends to seek revenge on Hindley.

At this point, Nelly interrupts her narrative and rises to go, remarking that the night is growing late. Lockwood says that he intends to sleep late the next day and wishes to hear the rest of her story now. He urges her to continue in minute detail.

Summary: Chapter VIII

Nelly skips ahead a bit in her story, to the summer of 1778, several months after the Lintons' visit and twenty-three years before Lockwood's arrival at the Grange. Frances gives birth to a baby boy, Hareton, but she dies not long afterwards, the strain of childbirth having aggravated her chronic consumption. Hindley assigns Nelly the task of raising the baby, as he takes no interest in the child. Miserable at Frances's death, Hindley begins to drink excessively and behaves abusively toward his servants—especially toward Heathcliff, who takes great pleasure in Hindley's steady decline. Catherine continues to spend time with Edgar Linton, and she behaves like a proper lady while with him. However, when she is with Heathcliff, she acts as she always has. One afternoon, when Hindley is out of the house, Heathcliff declares that he will stay home from the fields and spend the day with Catherine. She tells him ruefully that Edgar and Isabella are planning to visit. When Heathcliff confronts her about the amount of time she spends with Edgar, she retorts that Heathcliff is ignorant and dull. At that moment, Edgar enters—without Isabella—and Heathcliff storms away.

Catherine asks Nelly to leave the room, but Nelly refuses, having been instructed by Hindley to act as Catherine's chaperone in Edgar's presence. Catherine pinches her and then slaps her, and when Hareton begins to cry, she shakes him. Edgar, appalled at Catherine's behavior, attempts to restore order, and Catherine boxes his ears. Edgar is unable to cope with Catherine's unladylike temper and hurries out of the house. On his way out, however, he catches a last glimpse of Catherine through the window; lured by her beauty, he comes back inside. Nelly now leaves them alone and interrupts them only to tell them that Hindley has arrived home, drunk and in a foul temper. When she next enters the room, she can tell that Catherine and Edgar have confessed their love for one another. Edgar hurries home to avoid Hindley, and Catherine goes to her chamber. Nelly goes to hide little Hareton and takes the shot out of Hindley's gun, which he is fond of playing with in his drunken rages.

SUMMARY: CHAPTER IX

> *Heathcliff . . . shall never know how I love him . . . he's*
> *more myself than I am. Whatever our souls are made*
> *of, his and mine are the same. . . .*
>
> *(See* QUOTATIONS, *p. 55)*

Nelly is in the midst of hiding Hareton from Hindley when Hindley bolts in and seizes the boy. Stumbling drunkenly, he accidentally drops Hareton over the banister. Heathcliff is there to catch him at the bottom of the stairs.

Later that evening, Catherine seeks out Nelly in the kitchen and confides to her that Edgar has asked her to marry him, and that she has accepted. Unnoticed by the two women, Heathcliff listens to their conversation. Heathcliff hears Catherine tell Nelly that she cannot marry him because Hindley has cast him down so low; to marry him now would be to degrade herself. Heathcliff withdraws in a rage of shame, humiliation, and despair, and thus is not present to hear Catherine say that she loves him more deeply than anything else in the world. She says that she and Heathcliff are such kindred spirits that they are essentially the same person. Nonetheless, she insists, she must marry Edgar Linton instead.

That night, Heathcliff runs away from Wuthering Heights. Catherine spends the night outdoors in the rain, sobbing and searching for Heathcliff. She catches a fever, and soon she nears death. The Lintons take her to Thrushcross Grange to recuperate, and Catherine recovers. However, both Mr. and Mrs. Linton become infected and soon die. Three years later, Catherine and Edgar marry. Nelly transfers to Thrushcross Grange to serve Catherine, leaving Hareton in the care of his drunken father and Joseph, the only servant now remaining at Wuthering Heights.

Noticing the clock, Nelly again interrupts her narrative, saying that it is half past one, and that she must get some sleep. Lockwood notes in his diary—the same book in which he has set down Nelly's story—that he, too, will go to bed now.

ANALYSIS: CHAPTERS VI–IX

In this section, Nelly brings to conclusion the story of Heathcliff and Catherine's childhood, with Heathcliff leaving Wuthering Heights the night Catherine decides to marry Edgar Linton. In the climactic scene in which Catherine discusses with Nelly her decision to marry Edgar, Catherine describes the conflict between her love for Heathcliff and her love for Edgar. She says that she loves Edgar because he is handsome, rich, and graceful, and because he would make her the greatest lady in the region. However, she also states that she loves Heathcliff as though they shared the same soul, and that she knows in her heart that she has no business marrying Edgar. Nevertheless, her desire for a genteel and socially prominent lifestyle guides her decision-making: she would marry Heathcliff, if Hindley had not cast him down so low.

Heathcliff's emotional turmoil is due in part to his ambiguous class status. He begins life as a lower-class orphan, but is raised to the status of a gentleman's son when Mr. Earnshaw adopts him. He suffers another reversal in status when Hindley forces him to work as a servant in the very same household where he once enjoyed a life of luxury. The other characters, including the Lintons and, to an extent, Catherine—all upper-class themselves—prove complicit in this obliteration of Heathcliff's hopes. Inevitably, the unbridgeable gap in Catherine's and Heathcliff's social positions renders their fervent romance unrealizable on any practical level.

Nevertheless, the passion between the two lovers remains rooted in their hearts, impervious to external contingencies. The text consistently treats the love between Catherine and Heathcliff as an incontestable fact of nature. Nothing can alter or lessen it, and the lovers know this. Heathcliff and Catherine know that no matter how they hurt each other, they can be sure of never losing their shared passion and ultimate mutual loyalty. Catherine can decide to marry Edgar, certain that this outward act will have no effect on her and Heathcliff's inner feelings for one another. Similarly, it is in the knowledge of their passion's durability that Heathcliff later undertakes his cruel revenge.

CHAPTERS X–XIV

SUMMARY: CHAPTER X

Lockwood becomes sick after his traumatic experience at Wuthering Heights, and—as he writes in his diary—spends four weeks in misery. Heathcliff pays him a visit, and afterward Lockwood summons Nelly Dean and demands to know the rest of her story. How did Heathcliff, the oppressed and reviled outcast, make his fortune and acquire both Wuthering Heights and Thrushcross Grange? Nelly says that she does not know how Heathcliff spent the three years that he was away and that it was at this time that he apparently acquired his wealth. But she agrees to continue with her tale.

About six months after Catherine's marriage to Edgar Linton, Heathcliff returns home, surprising Nelly at Thrushcross Grange. When he comes indoors, Catherine becomes almost giddy with happiness at the sight of him, and their obvious affection for one another makes Edgar uncomfortable and jealous. Heathcliff has grown into a polished, gentlemanly, and physically impressive man, though some hint of savagery remains in his eyes. He announces that Hindley has invited him to stay at Wuthering Heights. This surprises both Catherine and Nelly, but Heathcliff tells Catherine that when he sought Nelly at Wuthering Heights earlier that day, he came across Hindley in a card game with his rough friends. Heathcliff joined them in the gambling, and, because his reckless bids seemed to bespeak a great wealth, Hindley excitedly invited him to return.

Catherine and Isabella begin to visit Wuthering Heights quite often, and Heathcliff returns the favor by calling at the Grange. Isabella begins to fall in love with Heathcliff, who, despite his obvious love for Catherine, does nothing to discourage her sister-in-law's affections. Nelly suspects that he harbors wicked and vengeful motives, and vows to watch him closely.

Summary: Chapter XI

Nelly travels to Wuthering Heights to talk with Hindley, but instead she finds Hareton, who throws stones at her and curses. Nelly learns from Hareton that Heathcliff has taught the boy to swear at his father, Hindley, and has forbidden the curate, who offered to educate Hareton, to set foot on the property. Heathcliff appears, and Nelly flees.

The next day, at the Grange, Nelly observes Heathcliff embracing Isabella. In the kitchen, Catherine demands that Heathcliff tell her his true feelings about Isabella. She offers to convince Edgar to permit the marriage if Heathcliff truly loves the woman. Heathcliff scorns this idea, however, declaring that Catherine has wronged him by marrying Edgar, and that he intends to exact revenge. Nelly informs Edgar of the encounter occurring between Catherine and Heathcliff in the kitchen, and Edgar storms in and orders Heathcliff off of his property. When Heathcliff refuses to leave, Edgar summons his servants for help. However, Catherine locks herself and the two men inside the kitchen and throws the key into the fire, forcing Edgar to confront Heathcliff without the help of additional men. Overcome with fear and shame, Edgar hides his face. Still, Catherine's taunts goad Edgar into striking Heathcliff a blow to the throat, after which Edgar exits through the garden. In terror of the larger and stronger

Heathcliff, Edgar hurries to find help, and Heathcliff, deciding that he cannot fight three armed servants, departs.

In a rage, Edgar declares that Catherine must choose between Heathcliff and himself. Catherine refuses to speak to him, locking herself in a room and refusing to eat. Two days pass in this way, and Edgar warns Isabella that if she pursues Heathcliff, he will cast her out of the Linton family.

SUMMARY: CHAPTER XII

At last, Catherine permits the servants to bring her food. Hysterical, she believes that she is dying, and cannot understand why Edgar has not come to her. She rants about her childhood with Heathcliff on the moors, and speaks obsessively about death. Nelly, worried that her mistress will catch a chill, refuses to open the window. Catherine manages to stumble to the window and force it open; from the window, she believes she can see Wuthering Heights. Catherine says that even though she will die, her spirit will never be at rest until she can be with Heathcliff. Edgar arrives and is shocked to find Catherine in such a weak condition. Nelly goes to fetch a doctor. The doctor professes himself cautiously optimistic for a successful recovery.

That very night, Isabella and Heathcliff elope. Furious, Edgar declares that Isabella is now his sister only in name. Yet he does not disown her, saying instead that she has disowned him.

SUMMARY: CHAPTER XIII

Edgar and Nelly spend two months nursing Catherine through her illness, and, though she never entirely recovers, she learns that she has become pregnant. Six weeks after Isabella and Heathcliff's marriage, Isabella sends a letter to Edgar begging his forgiveness. When Edgar ignores her pleas, she sends a letter to Nelly, describing her horrible experiences at Wuthering Heights. In her letter, she explains that Hindley, Joseph, and Hareton have all treated her cruelly, and that Heathcliff declares that since he cannot punish Edgar for causing Catherine's illness, he will punish Isabella in his place. Isabella also tells Nelly that Hindley has developed a mad obsession with Heathcliff, who has assumed the position of power at Wuthering Heights. Hindley hopes that somehow he will be able to obtain Heathcliff's vast fortune for himself, and he has shown Isabella the weapon with which he hopes to kill Heathcliff—a pistol with a knife attached to its barrel. Isabella says that she has made a terrible mistake, and she begs Nelly to visit her at Wuthering Heights, where she and Heathcliff are now living.

SUMMARY: CHAPTER XIV

Nelly grants Isabella's request and goes to the manor, but Edgar continues to spurn his sister's appeals for forgiveness. When Nelly arrives, Heathcliff presses her for news of Catherine and asks if he may come see her. Nelly refuses to allow him to come to the Grange, however, and, enraged, Heathcliff threatens that he will hold Nelly a prisoner at Wuthering Heights and go alone. Terrified by that possibility, Nelly agrees to carry a letter from Heathcliff to Catherine.

ANALYSIS: CHAPTERS X–XIV

Heathcliff, who seemed an almost superhuman figure even at his most oppressed, emerges in these chapters as a demonically charismatic, powerful, and villainous man, capable of extreme cruelties. Tortured by the depth of his love for Catherine, by his sense that she has betrayed him, and by his hatred of Hindley and the Linton family for making him seem unworthy of her, Heathcliff dedicates himself to an elaborate plan for revenge. The execution of this plan occupies much of the rest of the novel.

Though Heathcliff's first reunion with Catherine seems joyful, Nelly is right to fear his return, for he quickly exhibits his ardent malice, first through his treatment of the pathetic wretch Hindley, and then through his merciless abuse of the innocent Isabella. But though his destructive cruelty makes him the villain of the book, Heathcliff never loses his status as a sympathetic character. Although one can hardly condone his actions, it is difficult not to commiserate with him.

This ambiguity in Heathcliff's character has sparked much discussion among critics, who debate whether his role in the novel is that of hero or villain. In some sense, he fulfills both roles. He certainly behaves cruelly and harmfully toward many of the other characters; yet, because he does so out of the pain of his love for Catherine, the reader remains just as attuned to Heathcliff's own misery as to the misery he causes in others. The love between Catherine and Heathcliff constitutes the center of *Wuthering Heights* both thematically and emotionally, and, if one is to respond at all to the novel, it is difficult to resist sympathizing with that love. Correspondingly, as a participant in this love story, Heathcliff never becomes an entirely inhuman or incomprehensible character to the reader, no matter how sadistically he behaves.

Many scholars believe that Brontë intended her novel to be a moralizing, cautionary tale about the dangers of loving too deeply.

SUMMARY & ANALYSIS

If this is true, then one might argue that the book, in creating such charismatic main characters as Heathcliff and Catherine, defeats its own purpose. For instance, Isabella, though innocent and morally pure, never exerts the same power over the reader's imagination as Heathcliff and Catherine. As a result, it becomes unnervingly easy to overlook Isabella's suffering, even though her suffering would otherwise function as one of the novel's strongest pieces of evidence in its condemnation of obsessive passions. Similarly, Heathcliff suffers the ill treatment of characters who seem his intellectual and spiritual inferiors; thus when he seeks revenge on a brute such as Hindley, the reader secretly wishes him success. As a result, once again, Brontë's strong characterization of Heathcliff undermines any possible intent she might have had to warn her readers about the perils of an overly intense love.

In addition to exploring the character of Heathcliff as a grown man, this section casts some light on the character of Nelly Dean as a narrator. Her narrative has always shown certain biases, and throughout the book she harshly criticizes Catherine's behavior, calling her spoiled, proud, arrogant, thoughtless, selfish, naïve, and cruel. It is true that Catherine can be each of those things, but it also seems clear that Nelly is jealous of Catherine's beauty, wealth, and social station. It is important to remember that Nelly is not much older than Catherine and grew up serving her.

Some readers have speculated that Nelly's jealousy may also arise from a passion for Edgar Linton—whom she praises extravagantly throughout the novel—or even for Heathcliff, whom she often heatedly denounces. This section of the book offers some evidence for the latter view. For instance, when Catherine teasingly tells Heathcliff in Chapter X that Isabella has fallen in love with him, she does so by saying, "Heathcliff, I'm proud to show you, at last, somebody that dotes on you more than myself. I expect you to feel flattered." She then says, "Nay, it's not Nelly; don't look at her!" This comment suggests that Heathcliff looks at Nelly after Catherine's first statement. Perhaps in the past he has suspected Nelly of having feelings for him. Certainly, a reader might interpret Catherine's words in a different manner. Nevertheless, Catherine's comments substantiate the idea that Nelly's feelings for the other characters in the novel are deeper and more complicated than she reveals to Lockwood.

CHAPTERS XV–XX

SUMMARY & ANALYSIS

SUMMARY: CHAPTER XV

Four days after visiting Wuthering Heights, Nelly waits for Edgar to leave for church, and then takes the opportunity to give Heathcliff's letter to the ailing Catherine. Catherine has become so weak that she cannot even hold the letter, but nearly as soon as Nelly tells her that it is from Heathcliff, Heathcliff himself enters the room. Heathcliff and Catherine enter into a dramatic, highly charged conversation during which Catherine claims that both Heathcliff and Edgar have broken her heart. She says that she cannot bear dying while Heathcliff remains alive, and that she never wants to be apart from him. She begs his forgiveness. He says that he can forgive her for the pain she has caused him, but that he can never forgive her for the pain that she has caused herself—he adds that she has killed herself through her behavior, and that he could never forgive her murderer.

The church service over, Edgar reaches the house, but Catherine pleads with Heathcliff not to leave. He promises to stay by her side. As Edgar hurries toward Catherine's room, Nelly screams, and Catherine collapses. Heathcliff catches her, and forces her into Edgar's arms as he enters the room, demanding that Edgar see to Catherine's needs before acting on his anger. Nelly hurries Heathcliff out of the room, promising to send him word about Catherine's condition in the morning. Heathcliff swears that he will stay in the garden, wanting to be near her.

SUMMARY: CHAPTER XVI

At midnight, Catherine gives birth to young Catherine two months prematurely. She dies within two hours of giving birth. Nelly solemnly declares that her soul has gone home to God. When Nelly goes to tell Heathcliff what has happened, he seems to know already. He curses Catherine for the pain she has caused him, and pleads with her spirit to haunt him for the rest of his life. She may take any form, he says, and even drive him mad—as long as she stays with him. Edgar keeps a vigil over Catherine's body. At night, Heathcliff lurks in the garden outside. At one point, Edgar leaves, and Nelly permits Heathcliff a moment alone with the body. Afterwards, Nelly finds that he has opened the locket around her neck and replaced a lock of Edgar's hair with a lock of his own. Nelly twines Edgar's lock around Heathcliff's, and leaves them both in the locket.

Hindley is invited to Catherine's funeral but does not come, while Isabella is not invited at all. To the surprise of the villagers, Catherine is not buried in the Linton tomb, nor by the graves of her relatives. Instead, Edgar orders that she be buried in a corner of the churchyard overlooking the moors that she so loved. Nelly tells Lockwood that now, years later, Edgar lies buried beside her.

SUMMARY: CHAPTER XVII

Not long after the funeral, Isabella arrives at Thrushcross Grange, out of breath and laughing hysterically. She has come at a time when she knows Edgar will be asleep, to ask Nelly for help. Isabella reports that the conflict between Hindley and Heathcliff has become violent. Hindley, she says, tried to stay sober for Catherine's funeral, but could not bear to go. Instead, he began drinking heavily that morning. While Heathcliff kept a vigil over Catherine's grave, Hindley locked him out of the house and told Isabella that he planned to shoot him. Isabella warned Heathcliff about Hindley's plan, and when Hindley aimed his knife-gun out the window at Heathcliff, the latter grabbed it and fired it back at its owner's wrist, wounding Hindley. Heathcliff forced his way in the window, then beat Hindley severely. The next morning, Isabella reminded Hindley what Heathcliff had done to him the previous night. Hindley grew enraged, and the men began fighting again. Isabella fled to Thrushcross Grange, seeking a permanent refuge from Wuthering Heights.

Soon after her visit to Nelly, Isabella leaves for London, where she gives birth to Heathcliff's son, Linton. Isabella corresponds with Nelly throughout the following twelve years. Heathcliff learns of his wife's whereabouts, and of his son's existence, but he doesn't pursue either of them. Isabella dies when Linton is twelve years old.

Six months after Catherine's death, Hindley dies. Nelly returns to Wuthering Heights to see to the funeral arrangements, and to bring young Hareton back to Thrushcross Grange. She is shocked to learn that Hindley died deeply in debt, and that Heathcliff, who had lent Hindley large amounts of money to supply his gambling addiction, now owns Wuthering Heights. Heathcliff does not allow Hareton to return to Thrushcross Grange with Nelly, saying that he plans to raise him on his own. He also intimates that he plans to recover his son Linton at some point in the future. And so, Nelly tells Lockwood, Hareton, who should have lived as the finest gentleman in the area, is reduced to working for his keep at Wuthering Heights. A common, uneducated servant, he remains friendless and without hope.

Summary: Chapter XVIII

Young Catherine grows up at Thrushcross Grange, and by the time she is thirteen she is a beautiful, intelligent girl, but often strong-willed and temperamental. Her father, mindful of the tormented history of the neighboring manor, does not allow young Catherine off the grounds of Thrushcross Grange, and she grows up without any knowledge of Wuthering Heights, Heathcliff, or Hareton. She longs to visit the fairy caves at Penistone Crags, but Edgar refuses her request. He receives word one day, however, that Isabella is dying, and he hurries to London to take charge of young Linton. While he is gone, Catherine is left in Nelly's care, and she is able to escape the confines of the Grange.

She travels toward Penistone Crags but stops at Wuthering Heights, where she meets Hareton and takes an instant liking to him. She and Hareton spend a delightful day playing near the crags. Nelly arrives in pursuit of her charge, and tries to hurry her back to Thrushcross Grange. But Catherine refuses to go. Nelly tells Catherine that Hareton is not the son of the master of Wuthering Heights—a fact that makes the girl contemptuous of him—but she also reveals that he is Catherine's cousin. Catherine tries to deny this possibility, saying that her cousin is in London, that her father has gone to retrieve him there. Nelly, however, explains that a person can have more than one cousin. At last, Nelly prevails upon her to leave, and Catherine agrees not to mention the incident to her father, who might well terminate Nelly's employment in rage if he knew she had let Catherine learn of Wuthering Heights.

Summary: Chapter XIX

Edgar brings young Linton to the Grange, and Catherine is disappointed to find her cousin a pale, weak, whiny young man. Not long after he arrives, Joseph appears, saying that Heathcliff is determined to take possession of his son. Edgar promises that he will bring Linton to Wuthering Heights the following day.

Summary: Chapter XX

Nelly receives orders to escort the boy to the Heights in the morning. On the way, she tries to comfort Linton by telling him reassuring lies about his father. When they arrive, however, Heathcliff does not even pretend to love his son—he calls Linton's mother a slut, and he says that Linton is his property. Linton pleads with Nelly not to leave him with such a monster, but Nelly mounts her horse and rides away hurriedly.

ANALYSIS: CHAPTERS XV–XX

Wuthering Heights is, in many ways, a novel of juxtaposed pairs: Catherine's two great loves for Heathcliff and Edgar; the two ancient manors of Wuthering Heights and Thrushcross Grange; the two families, the Earnshaws and the Lintons; Heathcliff's conflicting passions of love and hate. Additionally, the structure of the novel divides the story into two contrasting halves. The first deals with the generation of characters represented by Catherine, Heathcliff, Hindley, Isabella, and Edgar, and the second deals with their children—young Catherine, Linton, and Hareton. Many of the same themes and ideas occur in the second half of the novel as in the first half, but they develop quite differently. While the first half ends on a note of doom and despair with Catherine's death and Heathcliff's gradual descent into evil, the novel as a whole ends on a note of hope, peace, and joy, with young Catherine's proposed marriage to Hareton Earnshaw.

In the first of the chapters in this section, we witness the event that marks the dividing line between the two halves of the novel: Catherine's death. The episodes surrounding her passing—her dramatic illness, her confrontation with Heathcliff, Heathcliff's conflict with Edgar, and Heathcliff's curse upon her soul to walk the earth after her death (contrasting immediately with Nelly's gentle claim that she at last rests in heaven) rank among the most intense scenes in the book. In fact, many readers view the second half of the novel, in which Catherine figures only as a memory, as a sort of anticlimax. While the latter chapters may never reach the emotional heights of the earlier ones, however, they remain crucial to the thematic development of the novel, as well as to its structural symmetry.

Young Catherine grows up sheltered at Thrushcross Grange, learning only in piecemeal fashion about the existence of Heathcliff and his reign at Wuthering Heights. Unbeknownst to her, Heathcliff's legal claim on the Grange (through his marriage to Isabella) may jeopardize her own eventual claim on it. Edgar Linton, however, painfully aware of this threat, searches for a way to prevent Heathcliff from taking the property. These events underscore the symbolic importance of the two houses. Wuthering Heights represents wildness, ungoverned passion, extremity, and doom. The fiery behavior of the characters associated with this house—Hindley, Catherine, and Heathcliff—underscores such connotations. By contrast, Thrushcross Grange represents restraint, social grace, civility, gentility, and aristocracy—qualities emphasized by the more mannered behavior of the Lintons who live there. The names of the two houses also bear out the contrast. While the adjective "wuthering" refers to violent storms, the thrush is a bird known for its melodious song, as well as being a symbol of Christian piety. In addition, whereas "Heights" evoke raw and imposing cliffs, "Grange" refers to a domestic site, a farm—especially that of a gentleman farmer. The concepts juxtaposed in the contrast of the two estates come into further conflict in Catherine's inability to choose between Edgar and Heathcliff. While she is attracted to Edgar's social grace, her feelings for Heathcliff reach heights of wild passion.

As the second generation of main characters matures, its members emerge as combinations of their parents' characteristics, blending together qualities that had been opposed in the older generation. Thus young Catherine is impetuous and headstrong like her mother, but tempered by the gentling influence of her father. Linton, on the other hand, represents the worst of both of his parents, behaving in an imperious and demanding manner like Heathcliff, but also remaining fragile and simpering like Isabella. Hareton appears as a second Heathcliff, rough and unpolished, but possessed of a strength of character that refuses to be suppressed, despite Heathcliff's attempts to stunt his development.

CHAPTERS XXI–XXVI

SUMMARY: CHAPTER XXI

Young Catherine despairs over her cousin's sudden departure from Thrushcross Grange. Nelly tries to keep up with the news of young Linton, quizzing the housekeeper at Wuthering Heights whenever she meets her in the nearby town of Gimmerton. She learns that Heathcliff loathes his sniveling son and cannot bear to be alone with him. She also learns that Linton continues to be frail and sickly.

One day, when young Catherine is sixteen, she and Nelly are out bird-hunting on the moors. Nelly loses sight of Catherine for a moment, then finds her conversing with Heathcliff and Hareton. Catherine says that she thinks she has met Hareton before and asks if Heathcliff is his father. Heathcliff says no, but that he does have a son back at the house. He invites Catherine and Nelly to pay a visit to Wuthering Heights to see the boy. Nelly, always suspicious of Heathcliff, disapproves of the idea, but Catherine, not realizing that this son is her cousin Linton, is curious to meet the boy, and Nelly

SUMMARY & ANALYSIS

cannot keep her from going. At Wuthering Heights, Heathcliff tells Nelly that he hopes Catherine and his son will be married some-day. For their part, the cousins do not recognize one another—they have changed much in three years—and because Linton is too sickly and self-pitying to show Catherine around the farm, she leaves with Hareton instead, all the while mocking the latter's illiteracy and lack of education. Heathcliff forces Linton to go after them.

At Thrushcross Grange the next day, Catherine tells her father about her visit and demands to know why he has kept her relatives secret. Edgar tries to explain, and eventually Catherine comes to understand his disdain for Heathcliff. But although Edgar gently implores her not to have any contact with Linton, Catherine cannot resist exchanging letters with the boy covertly. Nelly discovers the correspondence, and, much to Catherine's dismay, destroys Linton's letters to her. She then sends a note to Wuthering Heights requesting that Linton desist in his part of the correspondence. However, she does not alert Edgar to the young people's relationship.

SUMMARY: CHAPTER XXII

Edgar's health begins to fail, and, as a result, he spends less time with Catherine. Nelly attempts in vain to fill the companionship role formerly played by the girl's father. One winter day, during a walk in the garden, Catherine climbs the wall and stretches for some fruit on a tree. In the process, her hat falls off her head and down to the other side of the wall. Nelly allows Catherine to climb down the wall to retrieve it, but, once on the other side, Catherine is unable to get back over the wall by herself. Nelly looks for the key to the gate, and suddenly Heathcliff appears, telling Catherine that it was cruel of her to break off her correspondence with Linton. He accuses her of toying with his son's affections, and he urges her to visit Linton while he is away the following week. He claims that Linton may be dying of a broken heart. Catherine believes him and convinces Nelly to take her to Wuthering Heights the next morning. Nelly assents in the hope that the sight of Linton will expose Heathcliff's lie.

SUMMARY: CHAPTER XXIII

The following morning, Catherine and Nelly ride in the rain to Wuthering Heights, where they find Linton engaged in his customary whining. He speaks to Catherine about the possibility of marriage. Annoyed, Catherine shoves his chair in a fit of temper. Linton begins to cough and says that Catherine has assaulted him and has injured his already fragile health. He fills Catherine with guilt and requests that she nurse him back to health herself. After Nelly and Catherine ride home, Nelly discovers that she has caught a cold from traveling in the rain. Catherine nurses both her father and Nelly during the day, but, by night, she begins traveling in secret to be with Linton.

SUMMARY: CHAPTER XXIV

After Nelly recuperates, she notices Catherine's suspicious behavior and quickly discovers where she has been spending her evenings. Catherine tells Nelly the story of her visits to Wuthering Heights, including one incident in which Hareton proves to her that he can read a name inscribed above the manor's entrance: it is his own name, carved by a distant ancestor who shared it. But Catherine asks if he can read the date—1500—and he must confess that he cannot. Catherine calls him a dunce. Enraged, Hareton interrupts her visit with Linton, bullying the weak young man and forcing him to go upstairs. In a later moment of contrition, he attempts to apologize for his behavior, but Catherine angrily ignores him and goes home. When she returns to Wuthering Heights a few days later, Linton blames her for his humiliation. She leaves, but she returns two days later to tell him that she will never visit him again. Distressed, Linton asks for her forgiveness. After she has heard Catherine's story, Nelly reveals the girl's secret to Edgar. Edgar immediately forbids her from visiting Linton again, but he agrees to invite Linton to come to Thrushcross Grange.

SUMMARY: CHAPTER XXV

At this point, Nelly interrupts her story to explain to Lockwood its chronology: the events that she has just described happened the previous winter, only a little over a year ago. Nelly says that the previous year, it never crossed her mind that she would entertain a stranger by telling him the story. But she wonders how long he will remain a stranger, speculating that he might fall in love with the beautiful young Catherine. Lockwood confesses that he might, but says that he doubts his love would ever be requited. Besides, he says, these moors are not his home; he must return soon to the outside world. Still, he remains enraptured by the story, and he urges Nelly to continue. She obliges.

Young Catherine agrees to abide by her father's wishes and stops sneaking out to visit Linton. But Linton never visits the Grange, either—he is very frail, as Nelly reminds Edgar. Edgar worries over his daughter's happiness, and over the future of his estate. He says that if marrying Linton would make Catherine happy, he would

SUMMARY & ANALYSIS

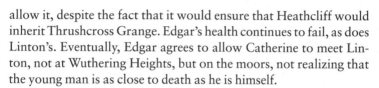

allow it, despite the fact that it would ensure that Heathcliff would inherit Thrushcross Grange. Edgar's health continues to fail, as does Linton's. Eventually, Edgar agrees to allow Catherine to meet Linton, not at Wuthering Heights, but on the moors, not realizing that the young man is as close to death as he is himself.

Summary: Chapter XXVI

When Catherine and Nelly ride to their meeting with Linton, they do not find him in the agreed-upon spot—he has not ventured far from Wuthering Heights. He appears frail and weak, but he insists that his health is improving. The youth seems nervous and looks fearfully over his shoulder at the house. At the end of their visit, Catherine agrees to meet Linton again on the following Thursday. On the way home, Catherine and Nelly worry over Linton's health, but they decide to wait until their next meeting before coming to any conclusions.

Analysis: Chapters XXI–XXVI

As Nelly tells Lockwood, her story has now nearly caught up with the present. Hareton was born in the summer of 1778; the first Catherine married Edgar in 1783 (a fact that can be extrapolated from Nelly's claim in 1801 to have been living at Thrushcross Grange for about eighteen years); and young Catherine was born in 1784, first met her cousins in 1797, and carried on her romance with Linton in the winter of 1800–1801, just over a year ago (see "Chronology"). The realization that Nelly has been narrating recent events should come as something of a surprise to the reader, to whom these events have seemed strange and distant. Now, both the reader and Lockwood realize that the story he has been hearing is not remote history, but bears on the present. Indeed, the events that Lockwood has just heard recounted may partially explain the interactions of the characters at Wuthering Heights when he first visited.

Apart from supplying important chronological information, these chapters largely help to further the generational drama, illustrating the similarities and differences between the first and second generations of main characters. Young Catherine's taunting of Hareton for his ignorance directly parallels the first Catherine's taunting of Heathcliff, just as Heathcliff's oppression of Hareton parallels Hindley's oppression of Heathcliff. In addition, these chapters demonstrate that Heathcliff accomplishes his revenge methodically, punishing his dead contemporaries by manipulating and bullying their children. By this point in the novel, revenge has supplanted love as the main force bearing upon Heathcliff's behavior. His acts take on a sense of urgency as he hurries to have young Catherine married to Linton before the boy dies. This plot evidences the way that Heathcliff makes a pawn of everyone—even his own son. Indeed, Heathcliff may despise Linton more than any other character in the novel. Worried that Linton will not outlive Edgar, Heathcliff hastens to secure his claim on Thrushcross Grange by uniting his son with Edgar's daughter.

Chapters XXVII–XXX

Summary: Chapter XXVII

During the next week, Edgar's health grows consistently worse. Worried for her father, young Catherine only reluctantly rides to her meeting with Linton on the moors. Nelly comes with her. The cousins talk, and Linton seems even more nervous than usual. He reveals that his father is forcing him to court Catherine, and that he is terrified of what Heathcliff will do if Catherine rejects him. Heathcliff arrives on the scene and questions Nelly about Edgar's health. He says that he worries that Linton will die before Edgar. Heathcliff asks Catherine and Nelly to walk back to Wuthering Heights, and, though Catherine reminds him that she is forbidden to do so by her father, she agrees because she is afraid of Heathcliff. Heathcliff seems full of rage toward Linton, who is practically weeping with terror. Once he has Nelly and Catherine inside Wuthering Heights, Heathcliff locks them inside the house and refuses to allow them to leave until Catherine has married Linton. He allows Catherine to leave the bedroom in which they are locked, but he keeps Nelly imprisoned there for five days. During this time, the only soul Nelly sees is Hareton, who is ordered to guard and attend her.

Summary: Chapter XXVIII

At last, the housekeeper, Zillah, frees Nelly from her imprisonment, telling her that the villagers in Gimmerton have spread the news that both Nelly and Catherine have been lost in Blackhorse Marsh. Nelly searches through the house until she finds Linton, who tells her that Catherine is locked away in another room. The two are now husband and wife. Linton gloats over this development, claiming that all of Catherine's possessions are now his, as Edgar is dying quickly. Fearing discovery by Heathcliff, Nelly hurries back to Thrushcross Grange. Here, she tells the dying Edgar that Catherine is safe and will soon be home. She sends a group of

SUMMARY & ANALYSIS

men to Wuthering Heights to retrieve Catherine, but they fail in their task. Edgar plans to change his will, placing Catherine's inheritance in the hands of trustees and thus keeping it from Heathcliff. He summons Mr. Green, his lawyer, to the Grange. Nelly hears someone arriving and believes it to be Mr. Green, but it is Catherine. Thus Edgar sees his daughter once more before he dies, believing that his daughter is happily married to Linton, and knowing nothing about her desperate circumstances. Shortly after Edgar's death, Mr. Green arrives, and dismisses all of the servants except Nelly. He tries to have Edgar buried in the chapel, but Nelly insists that he obey Edgar's will, which states that he wishes to be buried in the churchyard next to his wife.

Summary: Chapter XXIX

> "I got the sexton, who was digging Linton's grave, to remove the earth off her coffin lid, and I opened it. . . ."
> (See QUOTATIONS, p. 56)

Heathcliff appears at Thrushcross Grange shortly after the funeral in order to take young Catherine to her new home. He tells her that he has punished Linton for having helped her escape, and says that she will have to work for her keep at Wuthering Heights. Catherine angrily retorts that she and Linton are in fact in love, despite Linton's bad-temperedness, while Heathcliff has no one to love him. Thus no matter how miserable Heathcliff makes the young couple, Catherine says, they shall have the revenge of knowing that his cruelty arises from his greater misery.

As Catherine is packing her things, Nelly asks Heathcliff for Zillah's position at Wuthering Heights, desperate to remain with Catherine. But Heathcliff interrupts Nelly to tell her his astonishing deed of the day before. While the sexton was digging Edgar's grave, Heathcliff had him remove the earth from his beloved Catherine's, and he opened her coffin to gaze upon her face, which he says is still recognizable. Heathcliff asserts that Catherine will not crumble to dust until he joins her in the ground, at which point they will share the transformation together. He says that he forced the sexton to remove one whole side of her coffin—the side not facing Edgar—and that when he dies, he will require in his will that the corresponding side of his coffin be removed, so that he and Catherine might mingle in the earth. Nelly chastises him for disturbing the dead, and Heathcliff tells her that Catherine's ghost has tormented him every night

The young Catherine's manifestation of her mother's boldness, as well as Heathcliff's progressing revenge, bring to mind the older Catherine and the defiant marriage to Edgar with which she first sparked Heathcliff's wrath. Indeed, perhaps because of young Catherine's behavior, Heathcliff himself seems to become increasingly preoccupied with thoughts of the late Catherine. The horrifying spectacle of Heathcliff uncovering her grave and gazing upon her corpse's face, as well as his intense concern about the fate of Catherine's body, testifies to the extreme depth of his obsession. In a sense, Heathcliff's interest in the decomposition of his beloved is quite in keeping with the nature of their relationship. The text consistently describes their love not only in spiritual terms, but in material ones. Thus Catherine declares in Chapter IX, "Whatever souls are made of, his and mine are the same." Moreover, the relationship between Heathcliff and Catherine has come to be associated with the soil where it has been conducted; its fate becomes intertwined with that of the earth, as the narrative repeatedly links both Heathcliff and Catherine to the severe and wild moors, which frequently symbolize the unruly nature of their love.

These chapters give us insight not only into the story's main characters and their relationships, but also into the story's narrator, Nelly Dean. First, Nelly chooses to lie to Edgar about his daughter's condition as Edgar lingers near death, a well-meaning untruth that resembles her earlier lie to Linton, which she told en route to deliver him to Heathcliff. Just as she declared to Linton that his father was kind and generous, she now tells Edgar that his daughter is happily married. Nelly thus shows herself willing to lie and distort the truth in order to spare feelings and ease social situations. Nelly again displays a certain manipulative quality in a statement she makes outside the story, to Lockwood. She tells him that the young Catherine's last hope for salvation would be a second marriage, but that she, Nelly, is powerless to bring about such a union. This remark seems intended to express more than idle wishfulness. As the reader may recall, Nelly insinuates in Chapter XXV that Lockwood might fall in love with Catherine himself. At the time, the comment seemed nothing more than speculation. Yet now the reader can see that Nelly may be pursuing a plot to rescue her former mistress.

Indeed, Nelly's willingness to narrate the story to Lockwood in the first place may stem from this notion of saving Catherine. Nelly paints a far more flattering picture of young Catherine than she does of the girl's mother, even when they exhibit similar traits.

Nelly frequently emphasizes young Catherine's beauty, and she may subtly frame her story in a certain way so as to pique Lockwood's interest in the girl. Of course, this is merely one possible interpretation of the text, but again, it is extremely important to consider the motivations and biases of the character who narrates the story. One of the most impressive aspects of Emily Brontë's achievement in *Wuthering Heights* is her ability to include such finely drawn, subtle psychological portraits as that of Nelly Dean—many of whose most fascinating human qualities emerge only when one reads between the lines of her narration.

CHAPTERS XXXI–XXXIV

SUMMARY: CHAPTER XXXI

Lockwood, true to his word, travels to Wuthering Heights to end his tenancy at the Grange. He brings young Catherine a note from Nelly. Hareton first appropriates the note, but when Catherine cries, he gives it back to her. He has been struggling to learn to read and to acquire an education. Meanwhile, Catherine has been starving for books, as Heathcliff confiscated her collection. Catherine mocks Hareton's struggles to learn, angering him, but she admits that she does not want to hinder his education. Still, Hareton feels humiliated, and he throws his books into the fire.

Heathcliff returns, and on entering the house, he notes that Hareton has begun increasingly to resemble his aunt Catherine—so much so that he can hardly bear to see him. Lockwood passes a cheerless meal with Heathcliff and Hareton, and then departs the manor. As he leaves, he considers what a bleak place it is, full of dreary people. He muses further that it would have been like a fairy tale for young Catherine had she fallen in love with him and left Wuthering Heights for a more pleasant environment.

SUMMARY: CHAPTER XXXII

About six months later—Lockwood remained at the Grange until late winter, 1802, and it is now September, 1802—Lockwood writes in his diary that he has traveled again to the vicinity of the moors. There, he tries to pay a visit to Nelly at Thrushcross Grange, but discovers that she has moved back to Wuthering Heights. He rides to the manor, where he talks to Nelly and hears the news of the intervening months. Zillah has departed Wuthering Heights, and Heathcliff has given the position to Nelly. Catherine has admitted to Nelly that she feels guilty for having mocked Hareton's attempt to learn to read. One day, Hareton accidentally shoots himself, and is forced to remain indoors to recuperate. At first, he and Catherine quarrel, but they finally make up and agree to get along. To show her good will, Catherine gives Hareton a book, promising to teach him to read and never to mock him again. Nelly says that the two young people have gradually grown to love and trust each other, and that the day they are married will be her proudest day.

Summary: Chapter XXXIII

> *"In every cloud, in every tree—filling the air at night, and caught by glimpses in every object by day, I am surrounded with her image!"*
>
> *(See* Quotations, *p. 57)*

At breakfast the morning after Catherine gives Hareton the book, she and Heathcliff become embroiled in an argument over her inheritance and her relationship with Hareton. Heathcliff seizes her and nearly strikes her, but, looking into her face, he suddenly lets her go—apparently having seen something in her eyes that reminds him of her mother. Nelly speculates to Lockwood that so many reminders of the dead Catherine seem to have changed Heathcliff. In fact, he has confided to Nelly that he no longer has the desire to carry out his revenge on young Catherine and Hareton.

Summary: Chapter XXXIV

As time passes, Heathcliff becomes more and more solitary and begins to eat less and less, eventually taking only one meal a day. A few days after the incident at breakfast, he spends the entire night out walking, and he returns in a strange, wildly ebullient mood. He tells Nelly that last night he stood on the threshold of hell but now has reached sight of heaven. He refuses all food. He also insists that he be left alone—he wants to have Wuthering Heights to himself, he says. He seems to see an apparition before him, and to communicate with it, though Nelly can see nothing. Heathcliff's behavior becomes increasingly strange; he begins to murmur Catherine's name, and insists that Nelly remember his burial wishes. Soon, Nelly finds him dead. She tells Lockwood that he has since been buried, and that young Catherine and Hareton shall soon marry. They will wed on New Year's Day and move to Thrushcross Grange.

The young lovers now return to the house from outside, and Lockwood feels an overpowering desire to leave. He hurriedly exits through the kitchen, tossing a gold sovereign to Joseph on his way out. He finds his way through the wild moors to the churchyard, where he discovers the graves of Edgar, Catherine, and Heathcliff. Although the villagers claim that they have seen Heathcliff's ghost wandering about in the company of a second spirit, Lockwood wonders how anyone could imagine unquiet slumbers for the persons that lie in such quiet earth.

ANALYSIS: CHAPTERS XXXI–XXXIV

Unlike most Gothic romances, *Wuthering Heights* does not build to an intense, violent climax before its ending; rather, its tension quietly unravels as the inner conflict within Heathcliff gradually dissipates, his love for Catherine eroding his lust for revenge. Although the novel's happy ending is not possible until Heathcliff's death, his influence has become an ever less menacing one in the preceding days, and thus his demise does not constitute a dramatic reversal of the book's trends. As time passes, Heathcliff becomes increasingly obsessed with his dead love, and he finds reminders of her everywhere. He begins conversing with her ghost, and, after his climactic night on the moors—a night that we do not see or hear anything about, because Nelly was not there—a strange cheer comes over him, a happy premonition of his own impending death. Because he rejects all religious notions of the afterlife, Heathcliff does not fear death. Although the text frequently likens him to the Devil, he does not believe in hell, and his forced religious education as a child has caused him to deny the existence of heaven. His lack of religious belief leads him to refuse to allow Nelly to Christianize his death by calling for a priest. Rather, for Heathcliff, the end of life can mean only one thing: the beginning of his reunion with Catherine.

As Heathcliff anticipates a union in the afterlife, young Catherine and Hareton look forward to a shared life. Their love for one another seems not only to secure happiness for the future, but to redeem the miseries of the past. When young Catherine regrets aloud her mockeries of Hareton, she redeems not only her own past sins, but those of her mother, who behaved similarly toward Heathcliff—though without remorse. For his part, Hareton represents a final renewal for the manor of Wuthering Heights. He stands poised to inherit the estate, where his name is carved over the entrance, inscribed there by an earlier Hareton over three centuries before. Hareton's appropriation of the manor will signify the end of one cycle and the beginning of another, his very name marking the entry into a new era for Wuthering Heights. Finally, Catherine and Hareton together, as a unit, represent a resolution of past troubles. Together, they seem to manifest all of the best qualities of their parents and merge the various conflicting aspects of Wuthering Heights and Thrushcross Grange into a stronger whole. In essence, they embody the strength and passion of Wuthering Heights without its doomed intensity, and the civility and kindness of Thrushcross Grange without its cowardly snobbishness. Joined through their loving bond, the two estates will constitute a haven of warmth, hope, and joy.

Important Quotations Explained

1. But Mr. Heathcliff forms a singular contrast to his abode
    and style of living. He is a dark-skinned gypsy in aspect,
    in dress and manners a gentleman, that is, as much a
    gentleman as many a country squire: rather slovenly,
    perhaps, yet not looking amiss with his negligence, because
    he has an erect and handsome figure—and rather morose.
    Possibly, some people might suspect him of a degree of
    under-bred pride; I have a sympathetic chord within that
    tells me it is nothing of the sort: I know, by instinct, his
    reserve springs from an aversion to showy displays of
    feeling—to manifestations of mutual kindliness. He'll love
    and hate, equally under cover, and esteem it a species of
    impertinence to be loved or hated again—No, I'm running
    on too fast—I bestow my own attributes over-liberally
    on him.

This passage, from the first chapter and spoken in the voice of Lock-wood, constitutes the first of many attempts in the book to explain the mysterious figure of Heathcliff, his character and motivations. Outside of the novel, when critics and readers discuss *Wuthering Heights,* the same question arises repeatedly. How is Heathcliff best understood? We see here that the question of his social position—is he a gentleman or a gypsy?—causes particular confusion.

The situation of the reader, just beginning to enter into *Wuthering Heights* as a novel, parallels the situation of Lockwood, just beginning to enter into Wuthering Heights as a house. Like Lock-wood, readers of the novel confront all sorts of strange scenes and characters—Heathcliff the strangest of all—and must venture interpretations of them. Later illuminations of Heathcliff's personality show this first interpretation to be a laughable failure, indicating little beyond Lockwood's vanity. Lockwood, in claiming to recognize in Heathcliff a kindred soul, whom he can understand "by instinct," makes assumptions that appear absurd once Heathcliff's history is revealed. Lockwood, while he rather proudly styles himself a great misanthrope and hermit, in fact resembles Heathcliff very little. In the many misjudgments and blunders Lockwood makes in his early visits to Wuthering Heights, we see how easy it is to misinterpret Heathcliff's complex character, and the similarity between our own position and Lockwood's becomes a warning to us as readers. We, too, should question our instincts.

2. The ledge, where I placed my candle, had a few mildewed books piled up in one corner; and it was covered with writing scratched on the paint. This writing, however, was nothing but a name repeated in all kinds of characters, large and small—Catherine Earnshaw, here and there varied to Catherine Heathcliff, and then again to Catherine Linton. In vapid listlessness I leant my head against the window, and continued spelling over Catherine Earnshaw—Heathcliff—Linton, till my eyes closed; but they had not rested five minutes when a glare of white letters started from the dark, as vivid as spectres—the air swarmed with Catherines; and rousing myself to dispel the obtrusive name, I discovered my candle wick reclining on one of the antique volumes, and perfuming the place with an odour of roasted calf-skin.

QUOTATIONS

In this passage from Chapter III, Lockwood relates the first of the troubling dreams he has in Catherine's old bed. The quotation testifies to Lockwood's role as a reader within the novel, representing the external reader—the perplexed outsider determined to discover the secrets of Wuthering Heights. Upon Lockwood's first arrival at the house, no one answers his knocks on the door, and he cries, "I don't care—I will get in!" The same blend of frustration and determination has marked the responses of many readers and critics when facing the enigmas of *Wuthering Heights*.

The connection between Lockwood and readers is particularly clear in this passage. Catherine first appears to Lockwood, as she does to readers, as a written word—her name, scratched into the paint. When Lockwood reads over the scraped letters, they seem to take on a ghostly power—the simile Brontë uses is that they are "as vivid as spectres." Ghosts, of course, constitute a key image throughout the novel. In this instance, it is crucial to note that what comes back, in this first dream, is not a dead person but a name, and that what brings the name back is the act of reading it. We see that

Brontë, by using Lockwood as a stand-in for her readers, indicates how she wants her readers to react to her book; she wants her words to come vividly before them, to haunt them.

In this passage, one also can see an active example of *Wuthering Heights*'s ambiguous genre. The work is often compared to the Gothic novels popular in the late eighteenth century, which dealt in ghosts and gloom, demonic heroes with dark glints in their eyes, and so on. But Brontë wrote her book in the 1840s, when the fashion for the Gothic novel was past and that genre was quickly being replaced as the dominant form by the socially conscious realistic novel, as represented by the work of Dickens and Thackeray. *Wuthering Heights* often seems to straddle the two genres, containing many Gothic elements but also obeying most of the conventions of Victorian realism. The question of genre comes to a head in the appearances of ghosts in the novel. Readers cannot be sure whether they are meant to understand the ghosts as nightmares, to explain them in terms of the psychology of the characters who claim to see them, or to take them, as in a Gothic novel, as no less substantial than the other characters. Brontë establishes this ambiguity carefully. The "spectres" here are introduced within a simile, and in a context that would support their interpretation as a nightmare. Similarly subtle ambiguities lace Lockwood's account, a few pages later, of his encounter with the ghost of Catherine.

3. It would degrade me to marry Heathcliff now; so he shall never know how I love him; and that, not because he's handsome, Nelly, but because he's more myself than I am. Whatever our souls are made of, his and mine are the same, and [Edgar's] is as different as a moonbeam from lightning, or frost from fire.

Catherine's speech to Nelly about her acceptance of Edgar's proposal, in Chapter IX, forms the turning-point of the plot. It is at this point that Heathcliff leaves Wuthering Heights, after he has overheard Catherine say that it would "degrade" her to marry him. Although the action of *Wuthering Heights* takes place so far from the bustle of society, where most of Brontë's contemporaries set their scenes, social ambition motivates many of the actions of these characters, however isolated among the moors. Catherine's decision to marry Edgar Linton out of a desire to be "the greatest woman of the

QUOTATIONS

neighbourhood" exemplifies the effect of social considerations on the characters' actions.

In Catherine's paradoxical statement that Heathcliff is "more myself than I am," readers can see how the relation between Catherine and Heathcliff often transcends a dynamic of desire and becomes one of unity. Heterosexual love is often, in literature, described in terms of complementary opposites—like moonbeam and lightning, or frost and fire—but the love between Catherine and Heathcliff opposes this convention. Catherine says not, "I love Heathcliff," but, "I *am* Heathcliff." In following the relationship through to its painful end, the novel ultimately may attest to the destructiveness of a love that denies difference.

QUOTATIONS

4. "I got the sexton, who was digging Linton's grave, to remove the earth off her coffin lid, and I opened it. I thought, once, I would have stayed there, when I saw her face again—it is hers yet—he had hard work to stir me; but he said it would change, if the air blew on it, and so I struck one side of the coffin loose, and covered it up—not Linton's side, damn him! I wish he'd been soldered in lead—and I bribed the sexton to pull it away, when I'm laid there, and slide mine out too. I'll have it made so, and then, by the time Linton gets to us, he'll not know which is which!" "You were very wicked, Mr. Heathcliff!" I exclaimed; "were you not ashamed to disturb the dead?"

When Heathcliff narrates this ghoulish scene to Nelly in Chapter XXIX, the book enters into one of its most Gothic moments. Heathcliff, trying to recapture Catherine herself, constantly comes upon mere reminders of her. However, far from satisfying him, these reminders only lead him to further attempts. Heathcliff's desire to rejoin Catherine might indeed explain the majority of Heathcliff's actions, from his acquisition of Thrushcross Grange and Wuthering Heights, to his seizure of power over everyone associated with Catherine.

He tries to break through what reminds him of his beloved to his beloved herself by destroying the reminder, the intermediary. Readers can see, in the language he uses here, this difference between the objects that refer to Catherine and Catherine herself. When he opens her coffin, he does not say that he sees her again. Instead, he says, "I saw her face again," showing that her corpse, like her daughter or her portrait, is a thing she possessed, a thing that refers to her, but not the woman herself. It seems that, in this extreme scene, he realizes at last that he will never get through to her real presence by acquiring and ruining the people and possessions associated with her. This understanding brings Heathcliff a new tranquility, and from this point on he begins to lose interest in destruction.

5. That, however, which you may suppose the most potent to arrest my imagination, is actually the least, for what is not connected with her to me? and what does not recall her? I cannot look down to this floor, but her features are shaped on the flags! In every cloud, in every tree—filling the air at night, and caught by glimpses in every object by day, I am surrounded with her image! The most ordinary faces of men and women—my own features—mock me with a resemblance. The entire world is a dreadful collection of memoranda that she did exist, and that I have lost her!

In this passage from Chapter XXXIII, Heathcliff confesses to Nelly his inner state. What Nelly calls Heathcliff's "monomania on the subject of his departed idol" has now reached its final stage of development. In the passage in which Heathcliff describes his excavation of Catherine's grave, the reader gains insight into Heathcliff's frustration regarding the double nature of all of Catherine's "memoranda." While Catherine's corpse recalls her presence, it fails to substitute fully for it, and thus recalls her absence. Heathcliff's perception of this doubling comes through in his language. The many signs of Catherine show that "she did exist" but that "I have lost her." In the end, because his whole being is bound up with Catherine, Heathcliff's total set of perceptions of the world is permeated by her presence. Consequently, he finds signs of Catherine in the "entire world," and not just in localized figures such as her daughter or a portrait of Catherine.

QUOTATIONS

KEY FACTS

FULL TITLE
Wuthering Heights

AUTHOR
Emily Brontë

TYPE OF WORK
Novel

GENRE
Gothic novel (designed to both horrify and fascinate readers with scenes of passion and cruelty; supernatural elements; and a dark, foreboding atmosphere); also realist fiction (incorporates vivid circumstantial detail into a consistently and minutely thought-out plot, dealing mostly with the relationships of the characters to one another)

LANGUAGE
English (including bits of Yorkshire dialect)

TIME AND PLACE WRITTEN
In 1846–1847, Emily Brontë wrote *Wuthering Heights* in the parsonage of the isolated village of Haworth, in Yorkshire.

DATE OF FIRST PUBLICATION
1847

PUBLISHER
Thomas C. Newby

NARRATOR
Lockwood, a newcomer to the locale of Wuthering Heights, narrates the entire novel as an entry in his diary. The story that Lockwood records is told to him by Nelly, a servant, and Lockwood writes most of the narrative in her voice, describing how she told it to him. Some parts of Nelly's story are narrated by other characters, such as when Nelly receives a letter from Isabella and recites its contents verbatim.

POINT OF VIEW

Most of the events of the novel are narrated in Nelly's voice, from Nelly's point of view, focusing only on what Nelly can see and hear, or what she can find out about indirectly. Nelly frequently comments on what the other characters think and feel, and on what their motivations are, but these comments are all based on her own interpretations of the other characters—she is not an omniscient narrator.

TONE

It is not easy to infer the author's attitude toward the events of the novel. The melodramatic quality of the first half of the novel suggests that Brontë views Catherine and Heathcliff's doomed love as a tragedy of lost potential and wasted passion. However, the outcome of the second half of the novel suggests that Brontë is more interested in celebrating the renewal and rebirth brought about by the passage of time, and the rise of a new generation, than she is in mourning Heathcliff and Catherine.

TENSE

Both Lockwood's and Nelly's narrations are in the past tense.

SETTING (TIME)

The action of Nelly's story begins in the 1770s; Lockwood leaves Yorkshire in 1802.

SETTING (PLACE)

All the action of *Wuthering Heights* takes place in or around two neighboring houses on the Yorkshire moors—Wuthering Heights and Thrushcross Grange.

PROTAGONISTS

Heathcliff, Catherine

MAJOR CONFLICTS

Heathcliff's great natural abilities, strength of character, and love for Catherine Earnshaw all enable him to raise himself from humble beginnings to the status of a wealthy gentleman, but his need to revenge himself for Hindley's abuse and Catherine's betrayal leads him into a twisted life of cruelty and hatred; Catherine is torn between her love for Heathcliff and her desire to be a gentlewoman, and her decision to marry the genteel Edgar Linton drags almost all of the novel's characters into conflict with Heathcliff.

KEY FACTS

RISING ACTION

Heathcliff's arrival at Wuthering Heights, Hindley's abusive treatment of Heathcliff, and Catherine's first visit to Thrushcross Grange set the major conflicts in motion; once Heathcliff hears Catherine say it would "degrade" her to marry him, the conversation between Nelly and Catherine, which he secretly overhears, drives him to run away and pursue his vengeance.

CLIMAX

Catherine's death is the culmination of the conflict between herself and Heathcliff and removes any possibility that their conflict could be resolved positively; after Catherine's death, Heathcliff merely extends and deepens his drives toward revenge and cruelty.

FALLING ACTION

Heathcliff destroys Isabella and drives her away, takes possession of young Linton, forces Catherine and Linton to marry, inherits Thrushcross Grange, then loses interest in the whole project and dies; Hareton and young Catherine are to be engaged to be married, promising an end to the cycle of revenge.

THEMES

The destructiveness of a love that never changes; the precariousness of social class

MOTIFS

Doubles, repetition, the conflict between nature and culture

SYMBOLS

The moors, ghosts

FORESHADOWING

Lockwood's initial visit to Wuthering Heights, in which the mysterious relationships and lurking resentments between the characters create an air of mystery; Lockwood's ghostly nightmares, during the night he spends in Catherine's old bed, prefigure many of the events of the rest of the novel.

KEY FACTS

STUDY QUESTIONS

1. *Many of the names in* WUTHERING HEIGHTS *are strikingly similar. For example, besides the two Catherines, there are a number of Lintons, Earnshaws, and Heathcliffs whose names vary only slightly. What role do specific names play in Wuthering Heights?*

Names have a thematic significance in *Wuthering Heights*. As the second generation of characters gradually exhibits certain characteristics of the first generation, names come to represent particular attributes. The Earnshaws are wild and passionate, the Lintons tame and civilized; therefore, young Catherine Linton displays a milder disposition than her mother, Catherine Earnshaw. Linton Heathcliff becomes a mixture of the worst of both his parents. In other words, he possesses Heathcliff's arrogance and imperiousness, combined with the Lintons' cowardice and frailty. Names in *Wuthering Heights* also serve to emphasize the cyclic nature of the story. Just as the novel begins and ends with a Catherine Earnshaw, the name of Hareton Earnshaw also bookends an era; the final master of Wuthering Heights shares his name with a distant ancestor, whose name was inscribed above the main door in 1500.

2. *In many ways,* WUTHERING HEIGHTS *structures itself
    around matched, contrasting pairs of themes and of
    characters. What are some of these pairs, and what role
    do they play in the book?*

Matched and contrasting pairs form the apparatus through which
the book's thematic conflicts play out, as the differences between
opposed characters and themes force their way into action and
development. Some of the pairs include: the two manor houses,
Wuthering Heights and Thrushcross Grange; the two loves in
Catherine's life, Heathcliff and Edgar; the two Catherines in the
novel, mother and daughter; the two halves of the novel, separated
by Catherine's death; the two generations of main characters, each
of which occupies one half of the novel; the two families, Earnshaw
and Linton, whose family trees are almost exactly symmetrical; and
the two great themes of the novel, love and revenge. By placing these
elements into pairs, the novel both compares and contrasts them
to each other. The device of pairing serves to emphasize the book's
themes, as well as to develop the characters.

3.   *Analyze the character of Edgar Linton. Is he a
     sympathetic figure? How does he compare to
     Heathcliff? Is Catherine really in love with him?*

Edgar Linton is a kind, gentle, civilized, somewhat cowardly man
who represents the qualities of Thrushcross Grange as opposed to
the qualities of Wuthering Heights. Married to a woman whom he
loves but whose passions he cannot understand, Edgar is a highly
sympathetic figure after Heathcliff returns to Wuthering Heights.
The man finds himself in an almost impossible position, seeing his
wife obviously in love with another man but unable to do anything
to rectify the situation. Still, he proves weak and ineffectual when
compared to the strong-willed Heathcliff, and thus can exercise almost no claim on Catherine's mind and heart.

While the reader may pity Edgar and feel that morality may be on
his side, it is hard not to sympathize with the charismatic Catherine
and Heathcliff in their passionate love. It is impossible to think that
Catherine does not really love Edgar with some part of herself. Although she marries him largely because of her desire for his social
status, she seems genuinely drawn to his good looks, polished manners, and kind demeanor. But it is also impossible to think that her
feelings for Edgar equal her feelings for Heathcliff—compared with
her wild, elemental passion for Heathcliff, her love for her husband
seems frail and somewhat proper, like Edgar himself.

STUDY QUESTIONS

How to Write
Literary Analysis

The Literary Essay: A Step-by-Step Guide

When you read for pleasure, your only goal is enjoyment. You might find yourself reading to get caught up in an exciting story, to learn about an interesting time or place, or just to pass time. Maybe you're looking for inspiration, guidance, or a reflection of your own life. There are as many different, valid ways of reading a book as there are books in the world.

When you read a work of literature in an English class, however, you're being asked to read in a special way: you're being asked to perform *literary analysis*. To analyze something means to break it down into smaller parts and then examine how those parts work, both individually and together. Literary analysis involves examining all the parts of a novel, play, short story, or poem—elements such as character, setting, tone, and imagery—and thinking about how the author uses those elements to create certain effects.

A literary essay isn't a book review: you're not being asked whether or not you liked a book or whether you'd recommend it to another reader. A literary essay also isn't like the kind of book report you wrote when you were younger, where your teacher wanted you to summarize the book's action. A high school- or college-level literary essay asks, "How does this piece of literature actually work?" "How does it do what it does?" and, "Why might the author have made the choices he or she did?"

The Seven Steps
No one is born knowing how to analyze literature; it's a skill you learn and a process you can master. As you gain more practice with this kind of thinking and writing, you'll be able to craft a method that works best for you. But until then, here are seven basic steps to writing a well-constructed literary essay:

1. *Ask questions*
2. *Collect evidence*
3. *Construct a thesis*

4. Develop and organize arguments
5. Write the introduction
6. Write the body paragraphs
7. Write the conclusion

---

1. ASK QUESTIONS

When you're assigned a literary essay in class, your teacher will often provide you with a list of writing prompts. Lucky you! Now all you have to do is choose one. Do yourself a favor and pick a topic that interests you. You'll have a much better (not to mention easier) time if you start off with something you enjoy thinking about. If you are asked to come up with a topic by yourself, though, you might start to feel a little panicked. Maybe you have too many ideas—or none at all. Don't worry. Take a deep breath and start by asking yourself these questions:

- **What struck you?** Did a particular image, line, or scene linger in your mind for a long time? If it fascinated you, chances are you can draw on it to write a fascinating essay.

- **What confused you?** Maybe you were surprised to see a character act in a certain way, or maybe you didn't understand why the book ended the way it did. Confusing moments in a work of literature are like a loose thread in a sweater: if you pull on it, you can unravel the entire thing. Ask yourself why the author chose to write about that character or scene the way he or she did and you might tap into some important insights about the work as a whole.

- **Did you notice any patterns?** Is there a phrase that the main character uses constantly or an image that repeats throughout the book? If you can figure out how that pattern weaves through the work and what the significance of that pattern is, you've almost got your entire essay mapped out.

- **Did you notice any contradictions or ironies?** Great works of literature are complex; great literary essays recognize and explain those complexities. Maybe the title (*Happy Days*) totally disagrees with the book's subject matter (hungry orphans dying in the woods). Maybe the main character acts one way around his family and a completely different way around his friends and associates. If you can find a way to explain a work's contradictory elements, you've got the seeds of a great essay.

LITERARY ANALYSIS

At this point, you don't need to know exactly what you're going to say about your topic; you just need a place to begin your exploration. You can help direct your reading and brainstorming by formulating your topic as a *question,* which you'll then try to answer in your essay. The best questions invite critical debates and discussions, not just a rehashing of the summary. Remember, you're looking for something you can *prove or argue* based on evidence you find in the text. Finally, remember to keep the scope of your question in mind: is this a topic you can adequately address within the word or page limit you've been given? Conversely, is this a topic big enough to fill the required length?

Good Questions

"Are Romeo and Juliet's parents responsible for the deaths of their children?"

"Why do pigs keep showing up in Lord of the Flies*?"*

"Are Dr. Frankenstein and his monster alike? How?"

Bad Questions

"What happens to Scout in To Kill a Mockingbird*?"*

"What do the other characters in Julius Caesar *think about Caesar?"*

"How does Hester Prynne in The Scarlet Letter *remind me of my sister?"*

---

2. Collect Evidence

Once you know what question you want to answer, it's time to scour the book for things that will help you answer the question. Don't worry if you don't know what you want to say yet—right now you're just collecting ideas and material and letting it all percolate. Keep track of passages, symbols, images, or scenes that deal with your topic. Eventually, you'll start making connections between these examples and your thesis will emerge.

Here's a brief summary of the various parts that compose each and every work of literature. These are the elements that you will analyze in your essay, and which you will offer as evidence to support your arguments. For more on the parts of literary works, see the Glossary of Literary Terms at the end of this section.

ELEMENTS OF STORY These are the *what*s of the work—what happens, where it happens, and to whom it happens.

- **Plot:** All of the events and actions of the work.

- **Character:** The people who act and are acted upon in a literary work. The main character of a work is known as the *protagonist.*

- **Conflict:** The central tension in the work. In most cases, the protagonist wants something, while opposing forces (antagonists) hinder the protagonist's progress.

- **Setting:** When and where the work takes place. Elements of setting include location, time period, time of day, weather, social atmosphere, and economic conditions.

- **Narrator:** The person telling the story. The narrator may straightforwardly report what happens, convey the subjective opinions and perceptions of one or more characters, or provide commentary and opinion in his or her own voice.

- **Themes:** The main idea or message of the work—usually an abstract idea about people, society, or life in general. A work may have many themes, which may be in tension with one another.

ELEMENTS OF STYLE These are the *how*s—how the characters speak, how the story is constructed, and how language is used throughout the work.

- **Structure and organization:** How the parts of the work are assembled. Some novels are narrated in a linear, chronological fashion, while others skip around in time. Some plays follow a traditional three- or five-act structure, while others are a series of loosely connected scenes. Some authors deliberately leave gaps in their works, leaving readers to puzzle out the missing information. A work's structure and organization can tell you a lot about the kind of message it wants to convey.

- **Point of view:** The perspective from which a story is told. In *first-person point of view,* the narrator involves him or herself in the story. ("I went to the store"; "We watched in horror as the bird slammed into the window.") A first-person narrator is usually the protagonist of the work, but not always. In *third-person point of view,* the narrator does not participate in the story. A third-person narrator may closely follow a specific character, recounting that individual character's thoughts or experiences, or it may be what we call an *omniscient* narrator. Omniscient narrators see and know all: they can witness any event in any time or place and are privy to the inner thoughts and feelings of all characters. Remember that the narrator and the author are not the same thing!

- **Diction:** Word choice. Whether a character uses dry, clinical language or flowery prose with lots of exclamation points can tell you a lot about his or her attitude and personality.

- **Syntax:** Word order and sentence construction. Syntax is a crucial part of establishing an author's narrative voice. Ernest Hemingway, for example, is known for writing in very short, straightforward sentences, while James Joyce characteristically wrote in long, incredibly complicated lines.

- **Tone:** The mood or feeling of the text. Diction and syntax often contribute to the tone of a work. A novel written in short, clipped sentences that use small, simple words might feel brusque, cold, or matter-of-fact.

- **Imagery:** Language that appeals to the senses, representing things that can be seen, smelled, heard, tasted, or touched.

- **Figurative language:** Language that is not meant to be interpreted literally. The most common types of figurative language are *metaphors* and *similes,* which compare two unlike things in order to suggest a similarity between them—for example, "All the world's a stage," or "The moon is like a ball of green cheese." (Metaphors say one thing *is* another thing; similes claim that one thing is *like* another thing.)

---

3. CONSTRUCT A THESIS

When you've examined all the evidence you've collected and know how you want to answer the question, it's time to write your thesis statement. A *thesis* is a claim about a work of literature that needs to be supported by evidence and arguments. The thesis statement is the heart of the literary essay, and the bulk of your paper will be spent trying to prove this claim. A good thesis will be:

- **Arguable**. "*The Great Gatsby* describes New York society in the 1920s" isn't a thesis—it's a fact.

- **Provable through textual evidence**. "*Hamlet* is a confusing but ultimately very well-written play" is a weak thesis because it offers the writer's personal opinion about the book. Yes, it's arguable, but it's not a claim that can be proved or supported with examples taken from the play itself.

- **Surprising**. "Both George and Lenny change a great deal in *Of Mice and Men*" is a weak thesis because it's obvious. A really strong thesis will argue for a reading of the text that is not immediately apparent.

- **Specific**. "Dr. Frankenstein's monster tells us a lot about the human condition" is *almost* a really great thesis statement, but it's still too vague. What does the writer mean by "a lot"? *How* does the monster tell us so much about the human condition?

Good Thesis Statements

Question: In *Romeo and Juliet*, which is more powerful in shaping the lovers' story: fate or foolishness?

Thesis: "Though Shakespeare defines Romeo and Juliet as 'star-crossed lovers' and images of stars and planets appear throughout the play, a closer examination of that celestial imagery reveals that the stars are merely witnesses to the characters' foolish activities and not the causes themselves."

Question: How does the bell jar function as a symbol in Sylvia Plath's *The Bell Jar*?

Thesis: "A bell jar is a bell-shaped glass that has three basic uses: to hold a specimen for observation, to contain gases, and to maintain a vacuum. The bell jar appears in each of these capacities in *The Bell Jar*, Plath's semi-autobiographical novel, and each appearance marks a different stage in Esther's mental breakdown."

Question: Would Piggy in *The Lord of the Flies* make a good island leader if he were given the chance?

Thesis: "Though the intelligent, rational, and innovative Piggy has the mental characteristics of a good leader, he ultimately lacks the social skills necessary to be an effective one. Golding emphasizes this point by giving Piggy a foil in the charismatic Jack, whose magnetic personality allows him to capture and wield power effectively, if not always wisely."

LITERARY ANALYSIS

4. Develop and Organize Arguments

The reasons and examples that support your thesis will form the middle paragraphs of your essay. Since you can't really write your thesis statement until you know how you'll structure your argument, you'll probably end up working on steps 3 and 4 at the same time.

There's no single method of argumentation that will work in every context. One essay prompt might ask you to compare and contrast two characters, while another asks you to trace an image through a given work of literature. These questions require different kinds of answers and therefore different kinds of arguments. Below, we'll discuss three common kinds of essay prompts and some strategies for constructing a solid, well-argued case.

Types of Literary Essays

- **Compare and contrast**

    Compare and contrast the characters of Huck and Jim in The Adventures of Huckleberry Finn.

    Chances are you've written this kind of essay before. In an academic literary context, you'll organize your arguments the same way you would in any other class. You can either go *subject by subject* or *point by point*. In the former, you'll discuss one character first and then the second. In the latter, you'll choose several traits (attitude toward life, social status, images and metaphors associated with the character) and devote a paragraph to each. You may want to use a mix of these two approaches—for example, you may want to spend a paragraph a piece broadly sketching Huck's and Jim's personalities before transitioning into a paragraph or two that describes a few key points of comparison. This can be a highly effective strategy if you want to make a counterintuitive argument—that, despite seeming to be totally different, the two objects being compared are actually similar in a very important way (or vice versa). Remember that your essay should reveal something fresh or unexpected about the text, so think beyond the obvious parallels and differences.

- **Trace**

    Choose an image—for example, birds, knives, or eyes—and trace that image throughout Macbeth.

    Sounds pretty easy, right? All you need to do is read the play, underline every appearance of a knife in *Macbeth,* and then list them in your essay in the order they appear, right? Well, not exactly. Your teacher doesn't want a simple catalog of examples. He or she wants to see you make *connections* between those examples—that's the difference between summarizing and analyzing. In the *Macbeth* example above, think about the different contexts in which knives appear in the play and to what effect. In *Macbeth,* there are real knives and imagined knives; knives that kill and knives that simply threaten. Categorize and classify your examples to give them some order. Finally, always keep the overall effect in mind. After you choose and analyze your examples, you should come to some greater understanding about the work, as well as your chosen image, symbol, or phrase's role in developing the major themes and stylistic strategies of that work.

- **Debate**

    Is the society depicted in 1984 good for its citizens?

    In this kind of essay, you're being asked to debate a moral, ethical, or aesthetic issue regarding the work. You might be asked to judge a character or group of characters (*Is Caesar responsible for his own demise?*) or the work itself (*Is* JANE EYRE *a feminist novel?*). For this kind of essay, there are two important points to keep in mind. First, don't simply base your arguments on your personal feelings and reactions. Every literary essay expects you to read and analyze the work, so search for evidence in the text. What do characters in *1984* have to say about the government of Oceania? What images does Orwell use that might give you a hint about his attitude toward the government? As in any debate, you also need to make sure that you define all the necessary terms before you begin to argue your case. What does it mean to be a "good" society? What makes a novel "feminist"? You should define your terms right up front, in the first paragraph after your introduction.

    Second, remember that strong literary essays make contrary and surprising arguments. Try to think outside the box. In the *1984* example above, it seems like the obvious answer would be no, the totalitarian society depicted in Orwell's novel is *not* good for its citizens. But can you think of any arguments for the opposite side? Even if your final assertion is that the novel depicts a cruel, repressive, and therefore harmful society, acknowledging and responding to the counterargument will strengthen your overall case.

LITERARY ANALYSIS

5. WRITE THE INTRODUCTION

Your introduction sets up the entire essay. It's where you present your topic and articulate the particular issues and questions you'll be addressing. It's also where you, as the writer, introduce yourself to your readers. A persuasive literary essay immediately establishes its writer as a knowledgeable, authoritative figure.

An introduction can vary in length depending on the overall length of the essay, but in a traditional five-paragraph essay it should be no longer than one paragraph. However long it is, your introduction needs to:

- **Provide any necessary context.** Your introduction should situate the reader and let him or her know what to expect. What book are you discussing? Which characters? What topic will you be addressing?

- **Answer the "So what?" question.** Why is this topic important, and why is your particular position on the topic noteworthy? Ideally, your introduction should pique the reader's interest by suggesting how your argument is surprising or otherwise counterintuitive. Literary essays make unexpected connections and reveal less-than-obvious truths.

- **Present your thesis.** This usually happens at or very near the end of your introduction.

- **Indicate the shape of the essay to come.** Your reader should finish reading your introduction with a good sense of the scope of your essay as well as the path you'll take toward proving your thesis. You don't need to spell out every step, but you do need to suggest the organizational pattern you'll be using.

Your introduction should not:

- **Be vague.** Beware of the two killer words in literary analysis: *interesting* and *important*. Of course the work, question, or example is interesting and important—that's why you're writing about it!

- **Open with any grandiose assertions.** Many student readers think that beginning their essays with a flamboyant statement such as, "Since the dawn of time, writers have been fascinated with the topic of free will," makes them sound important and commanding. You know what? It actually sounds pretty amateurish.

- **Wildly praise the work.** Another typical mistake student writers make is extolling the work or author. Your teacher doesn't need to be told that "Shakespeare is perhaps the greatest writer in the English language." You can mention a work's reputation in passing—by referring to *The Adventures of Huckleberry Finn* as "Mark Twain's enduring classic," for example—but don't make a point of bringing it up unless that reputation is key to your argument.

- **Go off-topic.** Keep your introduction streamlined and to the point. Don't feel the need to throw in all kinds of bells and whistles in order to impress your reader—just get to the point as quickly as you can, without skimping on any of the required steps.

---

6. WRITE THE BODY PARAGRAPHS

Once you've written your introduction, you'll take the arguments you developed in step 4 and turn them into your body paragraphs. The organization of this middle section of your essay will largely be determined by the argumentative strategy you use, but no matter how you arrange your thoughts, your body paragraphs need to do the following:

- **Begin with a strong topic sentence.** Topic sentences are like signs on a highway: they tell the reader where they are and where they're going. A good topic sentence not only alerts readers to what issue will be discussed in the following paragraph but also gives them a sense of what argument will be made *about* that issue. "Rumor and gossip play an important role in *The Crucible*" isn't a strong topic sentence because it doesn't tell us very much. "The community's constant gossiping creates an environment that allows false accusations to flourish" is a much stronger topic sentence— it not only tells us *what* the paragraph will discuss (gossip) but *how* the paragraph will discuss the topic (by showing how gossip creates a set of conditions that leads to the play's climactic action).

- **Fully and completely develop a single thought.** Don't skip around in your paragraph or try to stuff in too much material. Body paragraphs are like bricks: each individual

LITERARY ANALYSIS

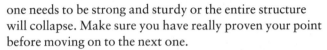

one needs to be strong and sturdy or the entire structure will collapse. Make sure you have really proven your point before moving on to the next one.

- **Use transitions effectively.** Good literary essay writers know that each paragraph must be clearly and strongly linked to the material around it. Think of each paragraph as a response to the one that precedes it. Use transition words and phrases such as *however, similarly, on the contrary, therefore,* and *furthermore* to indicate what kind of response you're making.

---

7. Write the Conclusion

Just as you used the introduction to ground your readers in the topic before providing your thesis, you'll use the conclusion to quickly summarize the specifics learned thus far and then hint at the broader implications of your topic. A good conclusion will:

- **Do more than simply restate the thesis.** If your thesis argued that *The Catcher in the Rye* can be read as a Christian allegory, don't simply end your essay by saying, "And that is why *The Catcher in the Rye* can be read as a Christian allegory." If you've constructed your arguments well, this kind of statement will just be redundant.

- **Synthesize the arguments, not summarize them.** Similarly, don't repeat the details of your body paragraphs in your conclusion. The reader has already read your essay, and chances are it's not so long that they've forgotten all your points by now.

- **Revisit the "So what?" question.** In your introduction, you made a case for why your topic and position are important. You should close your essay with the same sort of gesture. What do your readers know now that they didn't know before? How will that knowledge help them better appreciate or understand the work overall?

- **Move from the specific to the general.** Your essay has most likely treated a very specific element of the work—a single character, a small set of images, or a particular passage. In your conclusion, try to show how this narrow discussion has wider implications for the work overall. If your essay on *To Kill a Mockingbird* focused on the character of Boo Radley, for example, you might want to include a bit in your conclusion about how he fits into the novel's larger message about childhood, innocence, or family life.

- **Stay relevant.** Your conclusion should suggest new directions of thought, but it shouldn't be treated as an opportunity to pad your essay with all the extra, interesting ideas you came up with during your brainstorming sessions but couldn't fit into the essay proper. Don't attempt to stuff in unrelated queries or too many abstract thoughts.

- **Avoid making overblown closing statements.** A conclusion should open up your highly specific, focused discussion, but it should do so without drawing a sweeping lesson about life or human nature. Making such observations may be part of the point of reading, but it's almost always a mistake in essays, where these observations tend to sound overly dramatic or simply silly.

A+ ESSAY CHECKLIST

Congratulations! If you've followed all the steps we've outlined above, you should have a solid literary essay to show for all your efforts. What if you've got your sights set on an A+? To write the kind of superlative essay that will be rewarded with a perfect grade, keep the following rubric in mind. These are the qualities that teachers expect to see in a truly A+ essay. How does yours stack up?

- ✓ Demonstrates a thorough understanding of the book
- ✓ Presents an original, compelling argument
- ✓ Thoughtfully analyzes the text's formal elements
- ✓ Uses appropriate and insightful examples
- ✓ Structures ideas in a logical and progressive order
- ✓ Demonstrates a mastery of sentence construction, transitions, grammar, spelling, and word choice

Suggested Essay Topics

1. *Discuss the novel's narrative structure. Are the novel's narrators trustworthy? Why or why not? With particular reference to Nelly's story, consider what might be gained from reading between the lines of the narration. What roles do the personalities of the narrators play in the way that the story is told?*

2. *What role does social class and class ambiguity play in* Wuthering Heights? *To what extent is Heathcliff's social position responsible for the misery and conflict so persistent in the book?*

3. *Think about the influence of the physical landscape in the novel. What role do the moors play in the development of the story, and in the presentation of the characters? How does Catherine's abiding love of the moors help us to understand her character? What do the moors come to symbolize in the novel?*

LITERARY ANALYSIS

A+ Student Essay

> The characters in *Wuthering Heights* are enmeshed in
> a tangle of passionate sexual and familial relationships,
> many of them violent in nature. What is the relationship
> between love and revenge in the novel?

Love preoccupies nearly all of the characters in *Wuthering Heights*.
The quest for it motivates their actions and controls the development of the plot. Heathcliff, the character at the heart of the novel,
is the most impassioned lover. But if love drives him, the desire for
revenge drives him equally. Almost from the start, outrage at his
mistreatment at Catherine's hands inflames him, and after her marriage and eventual death, fury at being denied the chance to marry
her spurs him to take drastic, sometimes monstrous action. While
Heathcliff is perhaps best known for his love for Catherine, it is
his vengefulness that truly makes him memorable, in part because
that vengefulness produces such intense and mixed responses in us.
Paradoxically, Heathcliff's thirst for revenge makes us simultane-
ously loathe and admire him.

When Heathcliff comes home determined to seek revenge for
Catherine's betrayal, his behavior can be interpreted as at best child-
ish, and at worst cruel. Hindley may be half the man Heathcliff is,
but nevertheless, the two were raised as brothers. Moreover, whatever Hindley's childhood sins, he is now a broken man, a drunk and
a gambler. In light of these facts, we cannot help but look askance on
Heathcliff's willingness to coldly and methodically wrest Wuthering
Heights from him and to turn Hindley's own son, Hareton, against
him. Heathcliff treats Isabella equally unmercifully. She is a silly
woman, but an innocent one. Heathcliff, who thinks of her as nothing more than a pawn in his revenge game, treats her unfairly. And
his professed willingness to punish her for her brother's crimes may
strike us as slightly unhinged.

Heathcliff's quest for revenge is never seemly, but it becomes
downright grotesque as the years pass. After Catherine's death,
Heathcliff's vengefulness is less easy to understand: After all, the
woman he loves, the woman he wants to punish and impress, is
no longer around (at least in bodily form). As Heathcliff's motivations turn sour and confusing, his actions spiral downward, too.
In an attempt to get Edgar's estate, Heathcliff manipulates young

LITERARY ANALYSIS

Catherine and his own son, Linton, into an ill-advised romance and then forces the two to wed after kidnapping Catherine and holding her prisoner. Out of general ill will and a specific desire to punish Catherine's relatives, he abuses Hareton, the character who most closely resembles him. By denying the intelligent boy an education and keeping him in a state of servitude, Heathcliff re-creates the very ill treatment that was visited on him when he was young. It is a crime just as morally repugnant as is his manipulation of his own son.

Yet however bad Heathcliff's behavior, his desire for revenge makes him just as endearing as it does objectionable. First, while Heathcliff is a brute, he is an intelligent, capable brute. Those he controls are frailer and stupider than he, and part of us understands his desire to manipulate them as the natural dominance the strong feel over the weak. Second, his vengefulness arises from his deep love for Catherine. He is cruel not for cruelty's sake, but because the woman he loves has broken his heart. This is a familiar motivation in literature, and a difficult one to dismiss or condemn. After Catherine's death, even the shocking manifestations of Heathcliff's vengefulness can be interpreted as touching. Were his need for revenge to die with Catherine, it would suggest that his love for her was a temporary passion. Because his need for revenge only increases after her death, we are likely to conclude that his love for her is timeless, undying, and classically romantic. In one interpretation, the more outrageous and monstrous his actions are, the more clear, concrete, and passionate his love seems.

By the time Heathcliff dies, his hunger for revenge has also passed away. But that vengefulness is what keeps him alive in our minds, and makes him the most vivid of Brontë's fictional creations.

GLOSSARY OF LITERARY TERMS

ANTAGONIST

The entity that acts to frustrate the goals of the *protagonist*. The antagonist is usually another *character* but may also be a non-human force.

ANTIHERO / ANTIHEROINE

A *protagonist* who is not admirable or who challenges notions of what should be considered admirable.

CHARACTER

A person, animal, or any other thing with a personality that appears in a *narrative*.

CLIMAX

The moment of greatest intensity in a text or the major turning point in the *plot*.

CONFLICT

The central struggle that moves the *plot* forward. The conflict can be the *protagonist*'s struggle against fate, nature, society, or another person.

FIRST-PERSON POINT OF VIEW

A literary style in which the *narrator* tells the story from his or her own *point of view* and refers to himself or herself as "I." The narrator may be an active participant in the story or just an observer.

HERO / HEROINE

The principal *character* in a literary work or *narrative*.

IMAGERY

Language that brings to mind sense-impressions, representing things that can be seen, smelled, heard, tasted, or touched.

MOTIF

A recurring idea, structure, contrast, or device that develops or informs the major *themes* of a work of literature.

NARRATIVE

A story.

LITERARY ANALYSIS

NARRATOR

The person (sometimes a *character*) who tells a story; the *voice* assumed by the writer. The narrator and the author of the work of literature are not the same person.

PLOT

The arrangement of the events in a story, including the sequence in which they are told, the relative emphasis they are given, and the causal connections between events.

POINT OF VIEW

The *perspective* that a *narrative* takes toward the events it describes.

PROTAGONIST

The main *character* around whom the story revolves.

SETTING

The location of a *narrative* in time and space. Setting creates mood or atmosphere.

SUBPLOT

A secondary *plot* that is of less importance to the overall story but may serve as a point of contrast or comparison to the main plot.

SYMBOL

An object, *character,* figure, or color that is used to represent an abstract idea or concept. Unlike an *emblem,* a symbol may have different meanings in different contexts.

SYNTAX

The way the words in a piece of writing are put together to form lines, phrases, or clauses; the basic structure of a piece of writing.

THEME

A fundamental and universal idea explored in a literary work.

TONE

The author's attitude toward the subject or *characters* of a story or poem or toward the reader.

VOICE

An author's individual way of using language to reflect his or her own personality and attitudes. An author communicates voice through *tone, diction,* and *syntax.*

A Note on Plagiarism

Plagiarism—presenting someone else's work as your own—rears its ugly head in many forms. Many students know that copying text without citing it is unacceptable. But some don't realize that even if you're not quoting directly, but instead are paraphrasing or summarizing, *it is plagiarism* unless you cite the source.

Here are the most common forms of plagiarism:

- Using an author's phrases, sentences, or paragraphs without citing the source
- Paraphrasing an author's ideas without citing the source
- Passing off another student's work as your own

How do you steer clear of plagiarism? You should *always* acknowledge all words and ideas that aren't your own by using quotation marks around verbatim text or citations like footnotes and endnotes to note another writer's ideas. For more information on how to give credit when credit is due, ask your teacher for guidance or visit www.sparknotes.com.

Review & Resources

Quiz

1. What is inscribed above the entrance of Wuthering Heights?

    A. "Hindley Earnshaw, 1729"
    B. "1623"
    C. "Abandon all hope, ye who enter here"
    D. "Hareton Earnshaw, 1500"

2. What kind of countryside surrounds Wuthering Heights and Thrushcross Grange?

    A. Moorland
    B. Savannah
    C. Forest
    D. Grassy plains

3. What destination does the young Catherine have in mind when she leaves Thrushcross Grange for the first time?

    A. Wuthering Heights
    B. The fairy caves at Penistone Crags
    C. The nearby village
    D. London, where her cousin Linton lives

4. What is the name of the village near Wuthering Heights?

    A. Loch Crag
    B. Gimmerton
    C. Heatherton
    D. Purvey

5. In what region of England was Emily Brontë raised?

    A. Sussex
    B. Gloucestershire
    C. Yorkshire
    D. Warwickshire

6. Who plans to live at Thrushcross Grange at the end of the novel?

    A. Young Catherine and Hareton
    B. Lockwood
    C. Heathcliff
    D. Young Catherine and Linton Heathcliff

7. Over the course of the novel, which characters claim to see Catherine's ghost?

    A. Heathcliff, Hareton, young Catherine, and Joseph
    B. Edgar Linton and Heathcliff
    C. Joseph and Nelly Dean
    D. Lockwood and Heathcliff

8. On what day do young Catherine and Hareton plan to be married?

    A. New Year's Day
    B. The Ides of March
    C. The anniversary of Heathcliff's death
    D. Valentine's Day

9. Why does young Catherine climb over the garden wall?

    A. To escape from the Grange
    B. To meet with Linton
    C. To retrieve her hat, which fell off as she stretched for the fruit of a tree
    D. To escape her mother's ghost

10. Who raises Hareton during the early years of his life?

    A. Hindley
    B. Heathcliff
    C. Catherine
    D. Nelly

11. Who does Lockwood believe would have given young Catherine a fairy tale life, if only she would have fallen in love with him?

    A. Heathcliff
    B. Hareton
    C. Linton
    D. Lockwood

12. Which of the following characters dies first?

    A. Mrs. Earnshaw
    B. Mr. Earnshaw
    C. Mrs. Linton
    D. Edgar Linton

13. Which of the following characters dies last?

    A. Mr. Linton
    B. Catherine
    C. Heathcliff
    D. Linton

14. According to Heathcliff, when will Catherine's body decompose?

    A. When a hundred centuries have passed
    B. When Edgar Linton is finally cursed to hell
    C. Never
    D. When Heathcliff can join her in the earth

15. Where does Lockwood record Nelly's story?

    A. In a novel
    B. In his diary
    C. In the margins of his Bible
    D. In Catherine's diary

16. Which character speaks the words "I am Heathcliff!"

    A. Linton Heathcliff
    B. Hareton
    C. Heathcliff
    D. Catherine

REVIEW & RESOURCES

17. Which three names does Lockwood find inscribed in the window ledge near his bed at Wuthering Heights?

    A. Catherine Earnshaw, Catherine Linton, and Catherine Heathcliff

    B. Catherine Earnshaw, Hindley Earnshaw, and Hareton Earnshaw

    C. Isabella Linton, Isabella Heathcliff, and Isabella Earnshaw

    D. Nelly, Joseph, and Zillah

18. Where does Earnshaw originally find Heathcliff?

    A. London

    B. Boston

    C. Liverpool

    D. Gimmerton

19. Where is Catherine buried?

    A. In a churchyard overlooking the moors

    B. In the chapel

    C. Under a stone wall

    D. She is not buried, but cremated, and her ashes are scattered in the Thames.

20. At what age is Linton taken away from Thrushcross Grange by Heathcliff?

    A. Four

    B. Twenty

    C. Eleven

    D. Thirteen

21. At what age is Linton reunited with young Catherine?

    A. Twenty-two

    B. Nineteen

    C. Sixteen

    D. Forty-three

22. Whom does Hindley force to work as a servant in his home?

    A. Joseph
    B. Heathcliff
    C. Heathcliff's son, Linton
    D. Edgar Linton

23. Whom does Heathcliff force to work as a servant in his home?

    A. Hindley
    B. Catherine
    C. Hareton
    D. Isabella Linton

24. Where do Catherine and Heathcliff first become close?

    A. In the nursery at Wuthering Heights
    B. During Catherine's visit to Liverpool
    C. At Isabella Linton's birthday party
    D. On the moors

25. Whom does Edgar Linton sometimes forbid his daughter to visit?

    A. Linton Heathcliff
    B. Hareton Earnshaw
    C. Isabella Linton
    D. The evangelical servant Joseph

ANSWER KEY

1: D; 2: A; 3: B; 4: B; 5: C; 6: A; 7: D; 8: A; 9: C; 10: D; 11: D; 12: A;
13: C; 14: D; 15: B; 16: D; 17: A; 18: C; 19: A; 20: D; 21: B; 22: B;
23: C; 24: D; 25: A

Suggestions for Further Reading

ABRAMS, M.H., ed. "The Victorian Age (1830–1901)." In *The Norton Anthology of English Literature,* vol. 2, 891–910. New York: W. W. Norton, 1993.

ARMSTRONG, NANCY. "Emily Brontë: In and Out of Her Time." In *Brontë, Emily,* WUTHERING HEIGHTS, ed. William M. Sale, Jr., Norton Critical Edition (New York: W. W. Norton, 1990), 365–377. First published in *Genre* XV (Fall 1982): 243–264.

BLOOM, HAROLD, ed. *Emily Bronte's* WUTHERING HEIGHTS. New York: Chelsea House Publishers, 2007.

EAGLETON, TERRY. "WUTHERING HEIGHTS." In *Myths of Power: A Marxist Study of the Brontës,* 97–121. London: Palgrave Macmillan, revised edition 2005.

JONES, JUDY and WILLIAM WILSON. "A Bedside Companion to the Nineteenth-Century English Novel." In *An Incomplete Education,* 216–240. New York: Ballantine, 1987.

KERMODE, FRANK. "A Modern Way with the Classic." *New Literary History* 5 (1974): 415–434.

KIELY, ROBERT. "*Wuthering Heights*: Emily Brontë." In *The Romantic Novel in England,* 233–251. Cambridge, MA: Harvard University Press, 1972.

MILLER, J. HILLIS. "Emily Brontë." In *The Disappearance of God: Five Nineteenth-Century Writers,* 157–211. Cambridge, MA: Harvard University Press, 1963.

POOL, DANIEL. *What Jane Austen Ate and Charles Dickens Knew: From Fox Hunting to Whist—The Facts of Daily Life in Nineteenth-Century England.* New York: Simon & Schuster, 1994.

SparkNotes Literature Guides

Visit sparknotes.com for many more!